Contents

1: Health, Illness and Medicine
What is Health? What is
   Medicine?   4
Keeping Healthy   6
Organizing Medical Care   8

2: Medicine in Ancient Times
The Beginnings of
   Medicine   10
Greece and Rome   12
The 'Father of Medicine'   14

3: Medieval Medicine
Advances Under Islam   16
Mixing Medicine and
   Religion   18
Studying Body Structure   20

4: Scientific Beginnings
Experiment and
   Observation   22
From Harvey to Koch I   24
From Harvey to Koch II   26
Microscopes and Medicine   28

5: The 19th–20th Century
The Era of Drugs   30

Antibiotics and 'Wonder
   Drugs'   32
Advances in Surgery   34
X-Rays and Radiology   36

6: The Medical System Today
Check-ups and Tests   38
Electronic Eyes   40
Drug Treatments   42
Surgery, Transplants and
   Implants   44
Treating the Mind   46

7: Around the World
China and the East   48
India and the Middle East   50
Africa   52
The Americas   54

8: Medicine in the Future
The Coming Challenges   56
Healing the World   58

Glossary   60
Index   62

Words found in **bold** are explained
in the glossary on pages 60 and 61

1: HEALTH, ILLNESS AND MEDICINE

What is Health? What is Medicine?

▼ The peak of fitness: Nuba wrestlers from the Sudan. Their lifestyle and activities involve physical exertion which keeps the body in good shape.

▶ Changing fashions in health. In Queen Elizabeth I's time it was desirable to be pale (left). Nowadays a suntan is viewed as healthy and attractive. However, recent research has shown that tanning can be very harmful causing quite serious skin damage.

Health

Most people have good health for most of the time. But few people enjoy 'perfect health'. Health is more than just the absence of illness. There are always ways to become that little bit healthier, by eating better food, or taking more exercise.

A middle-aged person might seem to be in good health one day. Yet the next day he/she might collapse and die from a heart attack. Although outwardly healthy, inside the body, the heart had been **diseased** for many years.

Another person might seem to be fit and healthy, although perhaps slightly worried about some things, for instance money. He or she could become more and more depressed, and even try to commit suicide. Being healthy involves the mind as well as the body.

BELITHA

Information

LIBRARY

HISTORY
of
MEDICINE

STEVE PARKER

BELITHA PRESS

First published in Great Britain in 1991 by
Belitha Press Limited
31 Newington Green, London N16 9PU
Copyright © Belitha Press Limited and
Gareth Stevens, Inc. 1991
Illustrations/Photographs copyright © in this
format by Belitha Press Limited and Gareth
Stevens, Inc. 1991
All right reserved. No part of this book may be
reproduced or utilized in any form or by any
means, electronic or mechanical, including
photocopying, recording or by any information
storage and retrieval system, without permission
in writing from the Publisher.
ISBN 1 85561 057 4
Reprinted 1991, 1992
Printed in Hong Kong for Imago

KENT
ARTS & LIBRARIES

C030325028

British Library Cataloguing in Publication Data
CIP data for this book is available from the British
Library

Acknowledgements

Photographic credits:

Bibliothèque Nationale 16
Bodleian Library 11 left
Bridgeman Art Library 4 centre
J. Allan Cash 32
Mark Edwards 50 top
ET Archive 5, 43 left
Mary Evans Picture Library 13 bottom, 36 left
Werner Forman Archive 55
Format Photographers 50 bottom
Giraudon 25 bottom
Sally and Richard Greenhill 7 right, 38, 57
Robert Harding Picture Library 49
Hulton Picture Company 30 left, 33 right
Hutchison Library 47, 48, 51, 52, 53, 54 right,
    56, 58 left, 59
Imperial War Museum 33 left
The Independent 58 right
Magnum 4 left, 35 right, 42, 43 right
Mansell Collection 13 centre, 31
Massachusetts General Hospital 34

Master and Fellows of Trinity College,
    Cambridge 19 centre
National Portrait Gallery 25 top
Peter Newark's Western Americana 54 left
Österreichische National Bibliothek 17
Popperfoto 7 left, 35 top
Queen Mary's Hospital Roehampton 44 left
Ann Ronan Picture Library 13 left, 22 left, 27
    top
Science Museum 10, 11 right
Science Photo Library 32, 37, 39 left, 40, 41,
    43 top, 44 bottom
Ronald Sheridan's Photo Library 12, 14
John Watney Photo Library 19 top, 27 bottom,
    30 bottom, 39 right, 44 inset, 45
Wellcome Institute 8, 21, 22 right
Windsor Castle, Royal Library © 1990 Her
    Majesty The Queen 20
Zefa 4, 9

Illustrated by: James Field, Borin van Loon
and Eugene Fleury

Series editor: Neil Champion
Educational consultant: Dr Alistair Ross
Editor: Jill A. Laidlaw
Designed by: Groom and Pickerill
Picture research: Ann Usborne
Art director: Frances Mackay
Specialist consultant: Caroline Richmond

Did You Know?

Until quite recently in many countries, people with **mental illnesses** were called 'mad'. They were locked away, and doctors had no hope of treatment or cure. (In some regions this still happens today.) In recent years doctors have begun to understand how the mind works. Now they can successfully treat some kinds of mental illness.

◀ The horrors of surgical amputation, as portrayed by Rowlandson in 1793. The observers are keen to view the operation and show little interest in the poor patient!

WHO's Health

In 1948, the United Nations set up a special agency called the World Health Organization (WHO). Its aim is 'the attainment by all the peoples of the highest possible level of health.'

There are many WHO medical projects around the globe, including:

● The control of serious diseases such as **malaria** and **tuberculosis**.

● The improvement of medical services, by training doctors and nurses, and by providing the money to build hospitals, and buy drugs and medical equipment.

● Aiding victims of natural disasters such as famines and earthquakes. At these times diseases are more likely to spread.

● Giving advice to countries on setting up new medical services or improving their existing services.

Illness

Now and again, people become ill. There are many different ways in which a human body can go wrong. When things go wrong with the body, we try to put them right. This is where medicine comes in. Our ideas about health and illness shape our ideas about medicine.

Medicine

Doctors and other health workers such as dentists, **physiotherapists**, nurses and **osteopaths**, provide medical care. They find out what is wrong with us, and try to make us better, or at least ease our suffering. They treat us with medical drugs, operations and nursing care.

It has not always been like this. Through the ages, and around the world, people have had very different ideas about health, illness and medicine. Like science and art, medicine is part of the society and culture of the time. It changes with the times.

Keeping Healthy

Being Responsible

There are many aspects to keeping healthy. They include staying fit, active and in good physical condition, eating the correct foods, and not becoming overweight. Not smoking and not drinking too much alcohol are important as well. Some of these ideas are quite recent and change over the years.

There are other ways in which we can look after our bodies. It is important to tell the doctor about health problems, even small ones, because they might be an early warning sign of something more serious.

▲ Two different views of 'taking medicine'. In Europe or America we simply open a pill bottle and take one of the factory-made tablets. In rural Sumatra, South-East Asia, medicines are carefully prepared from local plants, to a recipe handed down through generations.

Handing Over Responsibility

Some people take little interest in their own bodies. They do not watch their weight, they eat too much and exercise too little. They may smoke, or drink to excess. When illness strikes, they leave it until the last minute before they visit their doctor. Then they expect to be made better. They rely on medicine to take care of them, rather than caring more for themselves.

This attitude has come partly from the success of our modern Western-style medicine. People in places like Europe, North America and

Australia are living longer, and having fewer diseases than ever before. We regularly hear about new 'wonder drugs' or advances in life-saving surgery. People may think: Why should I bother to look after myself? Medical care is so good that it will cure me.

The Cost of Medicine

Of course, this is not true. Modern Western-style medicine cannot cure everyone. There are many diseases such as certain cancers which have no cure. Also, modern medical care is very expensive. Some people cannot afford to pay for it. In countries where health care is run by the state, there are sometimes long waiting lists or shortages of drugs and hospital beds.

It makes more sense to prevent illness rather than treat it after it develops. As attitudes change, medicine is becoming more concerned with prevention. More people want to know how they can look after themselves, and how they can treat their own minor illnesses.

When We Need Medicine

Not all illnesses need medical care.

● If you go to bed very late one night, you probably feel tired the next day. You might be absent-minded and slow in your reactions. But most people would not call this being ill. By the day after, you will have recovered.

● If you develop a sore throat and a slight cough, you might be described as 'slightly ill'. You may be able to carry on as normal, though with some extra effort for a few days. A century or two ago, you might have been seen as quite healthy, if all you had was a slight cough!

● If you catch measles or influenza, you are definitely ill. You will need to stay in bed for several days and be cared for. There has been a decision: medical care is needed, and you have become a 'patient'.

◄ Smoking was once seen as sophisticated and 'cool'. Nowadays most people recognize its many bad effects on health, and they think it dirty and irresponsible – a self-inflicted health hazard.

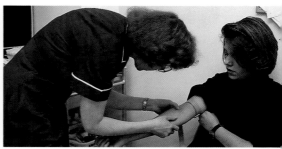

▲ A blood pressure check helps to reveal early warning signs of disease. It is part of the increasing swing away from treatment and towards prevention.

Organizing Medical Care

▶ A Chinese physician talks to his patient and carries out simple tests such as feeling the quality of the pulse. Each society has certain expectations of its medical practitioners.

Spending on Health

In the United States of America, the government spends 40% of their total budget on health care. Most of the money goes into childhood illnesses, diseases such as **diabetes**, mental illness, war veterans and people who are on Medicare and Medicaid; these are health insurance schemes for people who don't have much money, and old people.

▶ A medieval lecture in anatomy. Through the ages, training doctors has usually been a long and expensive process, from which the public expect good care in return.

In the past, there was less scientific knowledge about the human body and its ailments. Medical instruments and drugs were less complicated. Most doctors tried to give a wide range of medical care. There was little research into the causes and cures of disease.

As medical knowledge has expanded, so have systems of health care.

Levels of Care

Medical services are organized into several groups, or levels. No single doctor is an expert in all areas of medicine and there is not enough money to give every doctor new medical

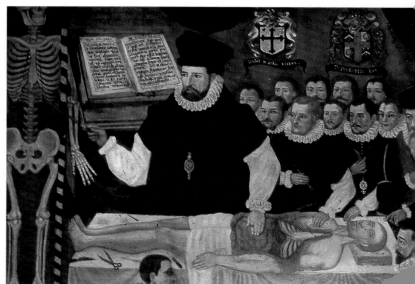

◄ On-the-spot care from fully trained ambulance staff.

Emergency Medical Care

When there is a serious accident or disaster, prompt medical care can save lives. The ambulance staff are trained in medical techniques and can give on-the-spot treatment, such as a fast-acting drug or a support for a broken limb. Members of the other emergency services, such as fire-fighters, are also trained in basic first aid.

equipment. It is more sensible to concentrate skills and facilities in hospitals.

Primary Care

The 'primary care' level involves the family doctor (general practitioner). This is the first person we are likely to see when we become ill. The family doctor works in a local area, knows many of the people personally, and is able to identify and treat common illnesses.

Secondary Care

The 'secondary care' level involves hospitals, specialists and their staff. When the family doctor is unable to pinpoint exactly what is wrong, or for more serious diseases, patients are advised to go to hospital or a specialist, for tests and treatments.

At the hospital are specialist doctors and nurses. Some concentrate on diseases that affect certain parts of the body, such as the cardiologist who treats heart problems, and the orthopaedic surgeon who deals with bones, muscles and joints. Other doctors specialize in health problems at a certain stage of life, such as paediatricians who care for children, and obstetricians who look after pregnant women and their developing babies.

There are also many other hospital staff. They include laboratory technicians, and technicians who operate the various pieces of equipment such as X-ray machines.

% OF GROSS NATIONAL PRODUCT

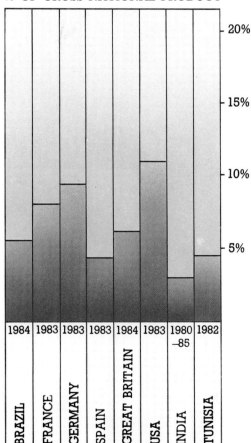

▲ The percentage of the **Gross National Product** spent on health care in selected countries, for a recent year.

2: MEDICINE IN ANCIENT TIMES

The Beginnings of Medicine

▲ Imhotep of Ancient Egypt was worshipped as a god.

▶ This stone relief sculpture from the Egyptian temple of Kom Ombo shows some of the **surgical instruments** in use at the time, including pincers and saws.

Humans live together in groups and help one another. Parents look after their children. When one person is hungry, another will share food. When one person falls ill, another tries to help. This is how medicine began. Some people became more knowledgeable than others – or at least, they seemed to be. They took on the role of looking after the sick, and became the first doctors.

Long before the beginnings of written history, we have evidence of medical care. The skeletons of some **Neanderthal** people had such deformed bones that, when alive, they would not have been able to feed and fend for themselves. Others must have cared for them.

Other skeletons from ancient burial grounds show signs of broken bones which had been 'set'. In other words, someone had positioned the broken parts so that they would grow back together again and heal well.

Trepanning

Clear signs of the first medical operations are skulls with neat holes in them. Some of these skulls are over 10,000 years old. The holes are the result of a process called trepanning. This

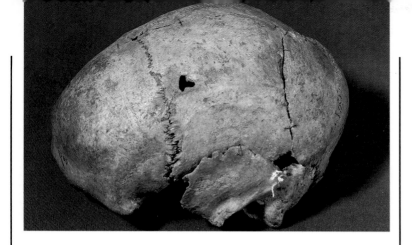

▲ A skull with a neat hole made by trepanning (trephining), some 6,000 years old (above left). The medieval thong-drill was one of many instruments used for this process (above).

was first carried out using stone cutters or scrapers to gouge through the skin, the muscle, and then bone, to the brain beneath. It was probably part of a magical ritual, to release evil spirits inside the head of the patient.

In Ancient Egypt

About 4,600 years ago, Imhotep lived in Ancient Egypt. He was a court sculptor, architect and doctor. People journeyed from far and wide to be treated by him. After his death, he was made into a god by his people. The sick flocked to his temples and worshipped statues of him, in the hope of being cured.

The Ancient Egyptians believed that each part of the body was watched over by a god. If disease developed in that part, then prayers, offerings and sacrifices to that god might bring about a cure. They also used medicines. They put mouldy bread on wounds – and we now know a type of bread-mould produces the **antibiotic** drug penicillin (page 32). They also used poppy sap, which contains pain-deadening chemicals, to relieve suffering.

Early Medical Writings

Two **papyrus** documents from Ancient Egypt carry writings about the medical techniques of the time. They both date from about 3,500 years ago.

The Smith papyrus gives information on how to set broken bones, how the pulse in the wrist can show the health of the heart, how to treat eye disease, how to stop bleeding by pressing on the wound, and many other procedures. Some are still in use today. This papyrus is probably a copy of an earlier version, perhaps 1,000 years older.

The Ebers papyrus contains information about 900 medications such as tannic acid for burns, and castor oil as a cure for constipation. It also gives chants and prayers for the gods, for specific illnesses. The god of physicians was Thoth, and the Ebers papyrus says 'He gives to the physicians skill to cure.' This papyrus also shows that the physicians prescribed special diets, massages and hypnosis for their patients.

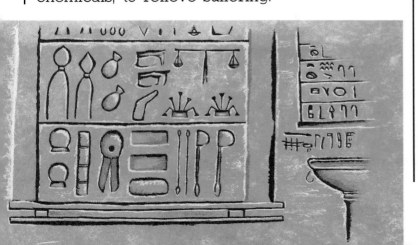

Greece and Rome

▲ The Roman hospitals, or valetudinaria, were clean and well-ordered places, where ill citizens and injured soldiers could rest and recover.

▲ False teeth from Ancient Rome, set in a gold bridge. Dental care was only one branch of the complex Roman health care system.

Greeks

For 800 years, from 2,600 to 1,800 the Ancient Greeks had a complex system of medicine.

Alcmaeon (born about 535 BC) is one of the first people known to have dissected (cut open and studied) dead people for medical purposes.

Empedocles (born about 492 BC) saw that the heart was connected into the network of **blood vessels**.

Aristotle (born about 384 BC) studied and dissected many animals. He was one of the most important figures in the history of science. He held a firm belief in the scientific method of making careful observations, doing experiments, and noting causes and their effects.

Celsus (born about 20 BC) wrote a medical encyclopedia *De re Medica* in eight volumes.

Roman Advances

The Romans improved the way medical services were organized. Doctors were taught and paid for by the state. The Romans began the first true hospitals, available to the general public. They built canals and aqueducts to supply fresh clean water, and disposed of sewage properly, since both dirty water and poor sewage disposal encourage disease.

The Great Galen

Galen (born about AD 130) spent much time dissecting animals, including monkeys. He applied his observations to the human body. He wrote hundreds of books describing the skeleton, muscles and nerves, and also the brain and the workings of the spinal cord. His teachings form the basis of the part of medicine known as **anatomy**, the study of the structure of the human body and its many organs.

Galen was also physician and **anatomist**. His many books summarized the medical knowledge of the day. After his time, and with the breakdown of the Roman Empire, medicine entered the **'Dark Ages'**. In arts and sciences little progress was made for several centuries.

▲ Asklepios treating Archinos, in the 4th century BC. Temples were built in his honour, where people visited and prayed to be healed.

Dreaming and Illness

Like the Egyptians, the Greeks mixed medicine with religion, magic and superstition. Many of the 'priest-physicians' worshipped a doctor whom they had made into a god, Asklepios (later called Aesculapius by the Romans). The patient came to one of the temples dedicated to him, and slept the night there. Next morning, he or she described any dreams to the priest, who interpreted the meaning of the dream and prescribed treatment.

◄ Galen (far left, above) was a great Roman physician, and one of the main founders of the science of anatomy. But many of his errors went unchallenged for centuries. Empedocles (far left, below), a philosopher from Ancient Greece, investigated the heart and blood vessels. Aristotle (left) was the chief founder of comparative anatomy, in which the parts of animals are described and compared, but it is doubtful that he studied the insides of human corpses.

The 'Father of Medicine'

Hippocrates of Cos was a doctor, surgeon, scientist and artist of Ancient Greece. He was born about 460 BC and spent many years on his birthplace the Greek island of Cos, in charge of the medical school and hospital there. His writings and teachings, and those of his colleagues and students, helped to lay the foundations of modern medicine.

Hippocratic Teachings

In Ancient Greece, medicine was bound up with religion and magic. Hippocrates and his colleagues tried to encourage a simple and sensible approach, that did not involve spirits and the supernatural world.

They taught that the doctor should examine the patient carefully and try to identify, or diagnose, the illness from the patient's condition, not from stories that others had told or religious 'signs'. The doctor should also look for causes of disease in the environment, in food or drink, or in the workplace, and give advice on prevention. The doctor should give treatment only when

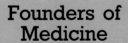

Founders of Medicine

No single person can be claimed as the founder of medicine. Hippocrates is probably the most famous, but many other Greeks and Romans helped to establish medicine as a science.

necessary. Hippocrates recognized rightly that the body has amazing powers to heal itself of less serious illnesses. Unnecessary treatment could have side-effects and make matters worse.

Treatment should be as simple as possible, such as a change in food. The doctor should predict the effects of treatment, so that the results can be judged later. He or she should keep good records of the patient's details and condition, so that these can be studied and learned from afterwards.

The Moral Code

Hippocrates and his colleagues devised guidelines about how doctors should think and behave. They wrote that a doctor's main aim is to help the patient, not to become rich or famous. Doctors should be sensible, thoughtful, well-trained, clean and modest. Also, when a doctor obtains personal information about a patient, this should be kept private and not told to others. This is called the Principle of Confidentiality and is still followed today.

▲ Hippocrates as he might have walked through the medical school and hospital on Cos. Besides teaching medicine he also encouraged good hygiene and high standards of moral and professional behaviour among trainee doctors.

Elements and Humours

Many philosophers of ancient times, including Aristotle, believed in the idea of four 'qualities' of life: hot, cold, wet and dry. These combined with four 'elements': earth, air, fire and water. If the combinations were out of balance in the body, illness resulted. After Hippocratic times, illness was linked to imbalance in the four 'humours' or liquids in the body: blood, phlegm, yellow bile and black bile. These ideas persisted for centuries, although we do not use them now.

3: MEDIEVAL MEDICINE

Advances Under Islam

In Europe, the period known as the Middle Ages lasted from about the 5th to about the 14th century. During this time there was little progress in any subject that today we would call science – this includes medicine. The skills of the Egyptians and Greeks and the organized public health of the Romans faded away.

In other parts of the world, medical knowledge was changing. As the Islamic Empire grew (7th century), its physicians developed and extended the works of the Greeks, which had been translated into Arabic.

The Black Death

The Black Death is a disease caused by **bacteria**. It has killed many millions of people throughout history. The illness is spread by the bites of fleas that have sucked blood from infected rats, and by droplets coughed up or sneezed out by people.

Between AD 551 and AD 555, plague swept across Europe and western Asia. At its height, in the city of Constantinople, the disease killed 10,000 people daily.

In 1346–50, plague returned to Europe and killed 25 million people. It was called the Black Death, partly because bleeding in the skin caused sufferers to come out in dark blotches.

Medical knowledge of the time was virtually powerless to halt the spread of plague. Today we can prevent its spread because we know it is carried by fleas, and it can be cured if antibiotic drugs are given without delay.

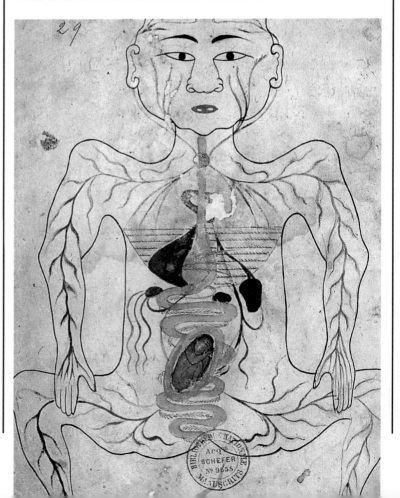

▶ A drawing of a pregnant woman showing the heart, blood vessels and other internal organs, prepared for a Persian prince during the 10th and 11th centuries.

◀ Arabic medical works were later taken up by the Europeans. This is a page from *Opere di Ippocrate e Galeno* which was translated from Arabic to Latin by Constantine (page 20).

Famous Physicians of Persia

In Persia the famed doctor Abu-Bakr Muhammad ibn Zakariyya Ar-Razi, also known as Rhazes, lived until AD 923. He gave one of the first descriptions of measles, and wrote many medical books, including the enormous encyclopedia *Kitab al-hawi*.

The physicians of this period were especially skilled at inventing and using new drugs. In fact our words such as *drug* and *alcohol* have Arabic origins. In AD 977 a hospital was set up in Baghdad (modern day Iraq), where more than 20 doctors carried out operations and ran a clinic for eye diseases.

In the early 11th century the Persian philosopher Ibn Sina, also known as Avicenna, practised medicine and produced numerous medical books. His great encyclopedia, *Canon of Medicine*, was based on Greek and Roman works. It was translated into other languages, including Latin, and became an important text in European medical schools for several centuries.

Progress in India

Farther east, new medical knowledge was also emerging. In the 5th century, the great Indian physician Susruta could choose from more than 100 surgical instruments for operations, and more than 700 medicinal plants for drug treatments. He rightly believed that mosquitoes spread malaria and rats spread plague. The skilled doctors of his time could set (reposition) broken bones if the skin was unbroken.

▲ Cosmas and Damian, two saints famous for healing. Many saints were credited with such powers, especially from the 4th to 6th centuries.

Mixing Medicine and Religion

▼ Monks pray for the souls of sick people in a medieval hospital. By asking for forgiveness and help from spiritual powers, they hoped to heal the patients.

Throughout history, in various parts of the world, medicine has been linked with religion. Changes in religious beliefs have affected medical knowledge, and the reverse has also happened. As pagan worship took over in Europe, and Christianity gradually spread to replace it by about the 12th century, this had various effects on how medicine was practised.

Body and Soul

On one hand, the Christian teachings of concern for others, and helping the feeble and sick, led to the founding of hospitals and caring centres for the poor. These were often run by monks, partly because they were among the few people who could read. Medical works, especially those of Aristotle and Galen, were in Latin, the language of scholars at that time.

On the other hand, religious views during this period said that some illnesses were caused by spirits or supernatural beings, such as a 'visit by the Devil'. Herbs, minerals and other medicines were part of the treatment, but it was also common to try to cure an illness by religious

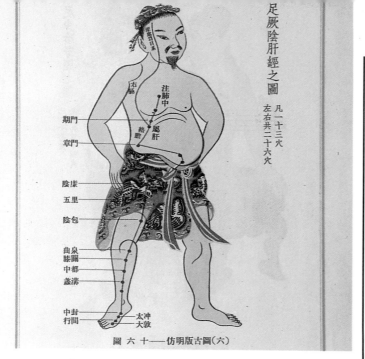

足厥陰肝經之圖

凡一十三穴
左右共二十六穴

圖 六 十——仿明版古圖（六）

means, such as prayers and offerings to cleanse the soul. The workings and ailments of the physical body were seen as less important. (Some people say that today we have gone too far the other way – see page 58.)

As a result, what we today call scientific medicine (page 22), progressed little. The knowledge of Galen and the Greeks was followed, but gradually it became confused and mixed with magic and superstition.

Eastern Progress

During the Dark Ages in Europe, medicine was developing in other regions such as India (page 50). In China, in about 620–630, Chen Ch'uan was probably the first physician to notice the typical symptoms of **diabetes**. The Chinese compiled a vast encyclopedia, *Pen T'saokang-mu*, over 10 centuries from the 6th century onwards, it describes more than 1,000 drugs.

◄ Acupuncture points (see page 49) in eastern belief and medicine make the connection between the mind and the body.

The Doctrine of Signatures

Many myths have grown up about the healing powers of plants. Some became included in the 'Doctrine of Signatures'. The doctrine says that if a plant resembles part of the human body it can be used to cure that part of an illness. For example, the flowers of eyebright have a blotchy, bloodshot appearance – and so they were recommended for red, sore eyes. The leaves of lungwort are rounded and speckled with white patches – and so they were advised for lung diseases. The root of meadow saffron looks like a foot swollen with **gout** – and so it should treat this condition. Indeed, there was sometimes an element of truth in these beliefs. Meadow saffron root is rich in colchicine, which acts as a painkiller.

▼ The resemblance of some plant parts to body parts, such as this ginseng root to the legs, encouraged the Doctrine of Signatures.

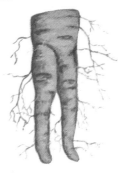

◄ Physicians and patients as depicted in a 13th-century work from Salerno. The illustration on the left shows heat therapy, while that on the right is of a leprosy sufferer.

19

Studying Body Structure

▲ Constantine of Carthage translated Arabic medical works into Latin at the Salerno medical school, around 1050–80. Latin was the language of educated people.

Art and Anatomy

Leonardo da Vinci lived from 1452–1519. His genius for both art and science led him to question the views of Galen. He was one of the first people to discuss openly that Galen could be wrong. But Leonardo's extraordinary anatomical drawings of humans and animals and his experiments were not published at the time. They made little impact on medical progress.

In the 3rd century BC, the Chinese medical book *Nei Ching* (Medicine of the Yellow Emperor) described the anatomy of the human body. However, in the West, little attention was paid to anatomy.

In the 9th century, in the Italian town of Salerno near Naples, a medical school grew up for the teaching of doctors and treatment of patients. The students studied anatomy and took examinations after five years. By the 12th century the Salerno medical school was famous throughout Europe and Asia. It slowly became less important as other centres of learning took over, such as Bologna in Italy, and then Montpellier in France.

Renaissance Medicine

During the early 14th century, the **Renaissance** period began in northern Italy. There was a rapid re-birth of the arts and sciences from their classical beginnings of many centuries ago before the Dark Ages. Painting, sculpture, architecture, music and philosophy all made great progress. So did medicine.

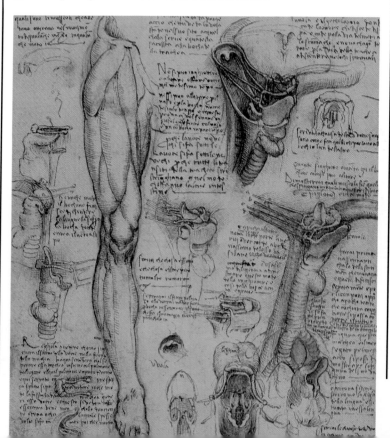

◀ Andreas Vesalius dissects the arm muscles.

The Padua School

Following Vesalius, the medical school at Padua produced many skilled physicians and anatomists.

● In the mid 16th century Gabriello Fallopio studied many parts of the body in minute detail. The fallopian tubes (**oviducts**) of the female sex organs are named after him.

● In the late 16th century Santorio Sanctorius, professor of medicine, began the serious study of body chemistry, and so helped to found the medical science of **physiology**. He invented devices for measuring body temperature and pulse rate.

Great artists of the period such as Michelangelo and Leonardo da Vinci studied the human form closely. Some dissected the bodies of people and animals and studied the muscles and other organs, to make their drawings more accurate.

The Work of Vesalius

During the 1530s Andreas Vesalius, a medical student from Brussels, realized the need to replace Galen's works with a more modern and accurate version. He went to the medical school in Padua, Italy, where he became professor of anatomy and surgery when only 24 years old, in 1538.

In 1543 Vesalius published his momentous book, *De Humani Corporis Fabrica*. He showed that in order to treat the body when ill, doctors needed to understand the structure and workings of the body when healthy. He exposed and corrected many of Galen's mistakes. Upon this firm footing, medicine entered a new era.

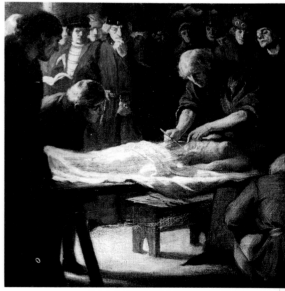

▲ Mundinus carries out a dissection at Bologna in 1318.

◀◀ Beautiful anatomical sketches from one of Leonardo da Vinci's many notebooks (opposite).

21

4: SCIENTIFIC BEGINNINGS

Experiment and Observation

During the 16th century, the pace of medical progress quickened in Europe. The printing press made books more widely available, researchers and doctors could share and learn from each other's work. The Renaissance inspired a desire for new knowledge and progress in the sciences. Then the **Industrial Revolution** allowed mass production of medical machines and equipment.

Only some medicine before this time had been scientific. It was based on careful observation, looking at causes and effects, developing theories about why things happen, and using experiments to test the theories. Now scientific methods were being used more widely, and with greater attention to detail.

Fernel and Paracelsus

Understanding of the body's anatomy and **physiology** was increasing all the time. Soon physicians began to apply this knowledge to diseases and their treatments. Jean François Fernel was professor of medicine at Paris. His

---

Occupational Diseases

Paracelsus recognized that health problems could be caused by a person's job, such as the condition now known as miner's lung. His work was continued by the Italian physician Bernardino Ramazzini in the late 17th century. Ramazzini was professor of medicine at Modena, Padua, and then Venice. He made a list of 40 jobs and trades, and illnesses such as cancers that were linked to them. His work was the foundation of 'occupational medicine'.

► Paracelsus (1493–1541) as portrayed in his work *Astronomica et astrologica* (1567) (right). Jean Fernel (1506–1588) depicted in a line engraving published in 1682 (far right).

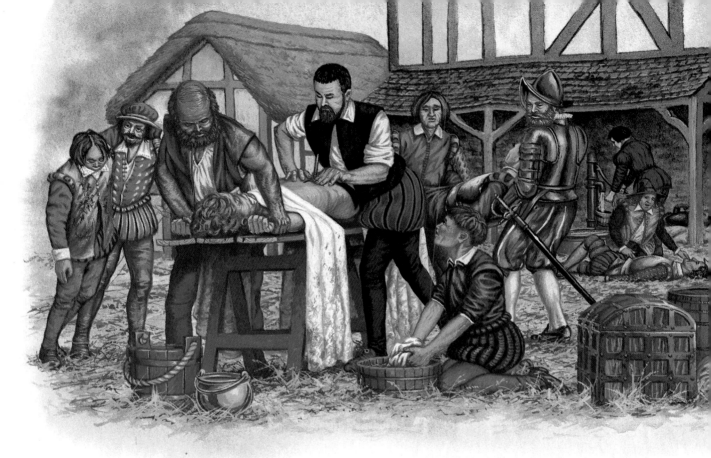

textbook *Universa Medicina* of 1554 broke new ground. The first part described human physiology and anatomy as the twin 'gateways to medicine'. The second part dealt with **pathology**, which is the study of human organs in their diseased state – another new idea. The third part of the book covered treatments.

Around the same time Philip Bombast von Hohenheim, known as Paracelsus, was travelling in Europe and treating patients. In 1526 he became professor at Basle University in Switzerland. Paracelsus introduced new chemical drugs, such as those containing mercury, sulphur, antimony, lead, iron and copper. He also treated his patients with courtesy and encouraged them to talk about their illness, in the manner of Hippocrates, which many physicians had forgotten. He had faith in the healing power of nature. Instead of the complicated prescriptions and potions of the time, he advised simple dressings for wounds and giving drugs one at a time.

▲ Ambroise (Andre) Pare was a foremost French army surgeon from 1536–45, and then surgeon-in-chief to four French kings in succession.

Infectious Diseases

Over the centuries, physicians had vague ideas about germs as the causes of certain diseases. In 1546, Italian physician Girolamo Fracastoro published his book *De Contagione at Contagiosis Morbis*. It was the first account of diseases that could be spread from person to person by 'minute bodies'. He mentions three ways of spreading – by touching parts of the ill person's body; by touching an object already touched by the ill person; and by being in the same place as the ill person. Fracastoro suspected that tiny germs existed, but there were no microscopes as yet so he could not prove his theories.

From Harvey to Koch I

▲ William Harvey applied the principles of hydraulics to his discovery of how the heart circulated blood. At the time many new machines were being developed, with pumps and tubes and flowing liquids, and these may have stimulated Harvey in his reasoning.

▶ Portraits of Thomas Sydenham (opposite, above) and Pierre Fauchard (opposite, below), who helped to establish dentistry.

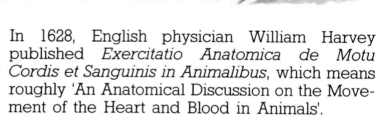

In 1628, English physician William Harvey published *Exercitatio Anatomica de Motu Cordis et Sanguinis in Animalibus*, which means roughly 'An Anatomical Discussion on the Movement of the Heart and Blood in Animals'.

Until Harvey's time, most physicians followed the old teachings of Galen (see p. 12). The heart was said to warm the blood, which was made in the liver and seeped from veins to **arteries** through the heart's dividing wall. The heartbeat and pulse were the result of the blood ebbing to and fro in the blood vessels, as it was enriched by a 'vital spirit'.

The Italian anatomists showed that blood could not seep through the heart's central wall, but they could not explain what happened instead. Harvey worked out that blood must flow continuously, in one direction only around the body, with the heart as the pump. This discovery had far-reaching effects on all fields of medicine.

Over the next two centuries, there were many momentous medical advances in Europe. People in other parts of the world had already made some of these discoveries, in certain cases centuries beforehand. But many of their findings had not led to further progress. The European advances are important because they were stepping stones that led to the scientific Western-style medicine we use today.

William Harvey

Harvey saw that the valves in the blood vessels resembled the valves being designed into **hydraulic** machines at the time, to control the flow of liquids. This is another example of medical progress being guided by the general scientific activity of the time. Eventually he settled on a theory in which blood went round the circulatory system, propelled by the heart's pumping. But Harvey could not say how blood got from the small arteries to small veins.

Thomas Sydenham

Sydenham has been called the 'English Hippocrates', and he had similarities with the great Greek physician. Sydenham emphasized the need to **diagnose** diseases correctly, and how to observe, care for and treat patients. He used cinchona bark (which contains the drug quinine) for malaria, extra iron for **anaemia**, and opium for great pain. In 1666 he published *Methodus Curandi Febres*, or 'The Method of Treating Fevers'. Sydenham believed that doctors should help and guide the body's own healing powers, and his notes on the case histories of patients are still admired today.

Pierre Fauchard

Chinese specialists had been filling and capping teeth with gold for many centuries. French surgeon Fauchard introduced the idea of dentistry as a medical speciality in its own right. In 1728 he produced *Le Chirurgien Dentiste, ou Traite des Dents* (The Surgeon Dentist, or Treatise of the Teeth).

Did You Know?

When we visit the doctor today, we expect to have our pulse taken. But this was not so in the past. John Floyer, an English physician, was one of the first Europeans to suggest that the pulse rate could be used to assess a patient's health. In 1707 he described his technique, and he even proposed a special watch to make accurate counts.

From Harvey to Koch II

Edward Jenner

Jenner was an English country doctor who developed the idea of **vaccination**. In Asia, it had been known for many centuries that people who were given a mild case of smallpox, by **inoculation** (putting the fluid from smallpox sores into their skin), would not get the serious and often deadly form of the infection. They were somehow **immune**. Jenner also knew of the popular belief that people who had cowpox, a much milder form of the disease caught from cattle, would not catch smallpox afterwards. In 1796 he inoculated a boy, James Phipps, with fluid from the sores on the hand of a dairymaid who had cowpox. A few weeks later he inoculated Phipps with smallpox. The boy did

not develop the disease. After many more experiments, Jenner published his work in 1798. Vaccination has since saved countless lives.

Thomas Hodgkin

In the early 1800s, Hodgkin became a physician at Guy's Hospital, London. His interest was pathology, the study of how the body parts respond and change during disease. Hodgkin helped to make the pathologist an important member of the medical team, whose work had practical value in treating illness, as well as being of purely scientific interest.

Louis Pasteur

Pasteur was a chemist and professor at Lille and Paris. In the mid 1800s, he showed that changes such as the **fermenting** of beer and the souring of milk were the result of tiny **animalcules** that came from the air or were carried on objects. This idea was soon applied to medicine; in the prevention of infection by Joseph Lister, and as the cause of disease by Robert Koch.

Florence Nightingale

In the mid 1800s, Florence Nightingale travelled to the Crimea and Turkey to help look after injured British soldiers who were fighting there. Her dedication and skill soon led to new nursing methods. On her return to London in 1860, she began a training school for nurses, with new standards of food, hygiene and health care in bright, clean, airy wards. She is regarded as the founder of the modern nursing profession.

Joseph Lister

Since the time of the Italian anatomists from Padua, surgery had made many advances. But the infections that wounds carried still killed many patients. During the mid 1800s, Lister was professor of surgery at Glasgow, Edinburgh and then London. He developed Pasteur's work and tried to prevent the **microbes** from infecting patients, by the use of chemicals called **anti-septics**, which killed the 'germs'. In 1867 he published his work, and surgery soon became a much safer procedure.

Robert Koch

A German physician, Robert Koch, established the branch of medicine known as **bacteriology** in the late 1800s. He continued Pasteur's work and showed that certain types of microbes, especially bacteria, are the cause of many infectious diseases. He studied **anthrax** and in 1882 discovered the bacteria that causes the widespread and much-feared disease tuberculosis. He also developed ways of grouping and naming bacteria and growing them under special **culture** conditions in the laboratory.

Micro-scopes and Medicine

In the year that William Harvey published his great work (1628), Marcello Malpighi was born in Italy. He was professor at Bologna and then Pisa, and he was the first anatomist to use a microscope.

Galileo had made an early type of microscope in the previous century. Malpighi used an improved version to study many parts of the body. In 1661 he saw the **capillaries** that connected arteries and veins, forming a complete circuit for the blood – his specimen was a frog's lung! Malpighi also continued work on the development of eggs, helping to establish the science of **embryology**.

▲ Malpighi studies the microscopic structure of frog tissues. The malpighian tubules, tiny tubes in the kidneys of animals and humans which help to rid the body of wastes, are named after him.

The Draper of Delft

About the same time as Malpighi, Antony van Leeuwenhoek was peering through a simple home-made microscope of his own design. A draper by trade from Delft, Holland, he had no proper scientific or medical training. Yet he manufactured his own lenses and saw and

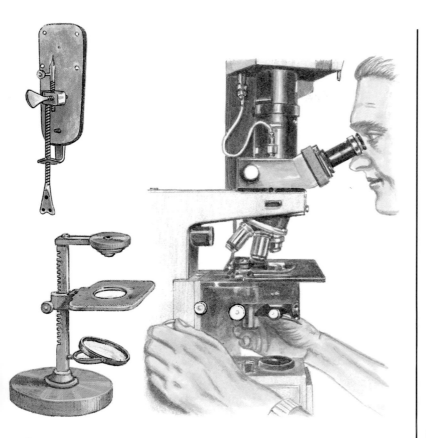

◄ Microscopes developed rapidly after their invention: simple early models like van Leeuwenhoek's first microscope were only 8 centimetres tall (far left). Below left we see a later model by van Leenwenhoek. Modern light microscopes (left) have adjustable lenses for different magnifications. The discovery of cells in the body opened the way for a whole new field of medicine.

described the red **cells** of the blood, the fibres of muscles, and the **sperm** from the male sex organs. In 1683 he drew diagrams of harmless bacteria from his own mouth.

Gradually medicine took up the microscope to help **diagnosis**, to discover the causes and effects of disease. In the late 19th century improvements to microscope equipment began a new era in microscopic medicine.

The Cell Theory

In the early and mid 19th century, biologists were developing the theory that all living things were composed of tiny building blocks, which they called cells. Medicine soon applied this knowledge to the human body.

Jakob Henle, studied many human organs under the microscope and helped to show that they were indeed made of cells. In the mid 19th century he unravelled the **micro-structure** of the kidney, he also worked on the eye and brain, and the muscle layers in the walls of arteries.

Cellular Pathology

Rudolf Virchow was a Prussian statesman, anthropologist and pathologist. Like Henle, he showed that body **tissues** were composed of **cells** and their products. His principle was that 'every cell comes from a cell'. Virchow proposed that every cell in the body had been produced from a cell. This process could be traced back through the body's development, to a single first cell – the fertilized egg.

Virchow extended his work into medicine by showing that diseases are the result of cells working wrongly or being destroyed. These changes could be seen through the microscope. His ideas led to the founding of the branch of medicine known as **cellular pathology**. Today, this is a vital part of the study and treatment of many diseases, such as cancers.

5: THE 19TH–20TH CENTURY

The Era of Drugs

▼ Frederick Banting and Charles Best developed treatment for the condition of diabetes by injections of the hormone insulin. Here they are joined by their 'patient', the first dog to be successfully treated as part of the animal testing of insulin, in 1921.

In the year 1900, four important discoveries were made. The American military surgeon Walter Reed led a team that showed the disease yellow fever was not due to bacterial infection spread by personal contact. It was spread by the bite of a certain mosquito, *Aedes aegypti*. The next year Reed identified the **virus** responsible. Within a few years, mosquito-breeding areas were being cleared in southern North America, Central and South America, and Africa, and the disease was in decline.

Scottish military officer William Leishman discovered that the tropical disease kala-azar was also spread by insects, in this case sandflies. It was caused by a tiny one-celled animal that multiplied in the blood. We now know this disease as leishmaniasis.

▶ As psychiatric medicine progressed, many new drug therapies were developed. This patient is being helped by art therapy, where painting and drawing are an aid to recovery.

Blood Groups

Also in 1900, Austrian scientist and doctor Karl Landsteiner demonstrated that not all human blood was the same. He discovered at least three types, which we call A, B and O, and soon after identified the AB type. Landsteiner also unravelled the Rhesus blood types, in about 1940. This pioneering work on blood groups made blood transfusions and surgery immeasurably safer.

Mental Illness

In 1900 Sigmund Freud, a Viennese physician, published his work *Die Traumdeutung* (The Interpretation of Dreams). Freud helped to found **psychiatry** (page 46).

Patterns of Progress

Year by year, more discoveries were made. Through the first half of the century, the pattern of progress gradually changed. Medical research became more complex and expensive. The era of the lone pioneering doctor, making far-reaching discoveries in a home surgery, was drawing to a close. Teams of researchers, using sophisticated equipment, laboratories and hospital facilities, became more common.

▲ Walter Reed makes medical notes at his 'battleground' against yellow fever, the Panama Canal construction site.

Modern Drug Therapy

In 1908, German bacteriologist Paul Ehrlich was awarded the **Nobel Prize** for Medicine. Ehrlich had studied the way the body develops resistance to certain infections after it has suffered from them once – the process of immunity. Working with Emil von Behring, he developed an **immunization** method for the children's disease **diphtheria**.

Then, in 1910, Ehrlich introduced the laboratory-made drug Salvarsan (arsphenamine) to treat the disease syphilis. This marked the beginnings of modern drug therapy, where new drugs are made chemically, rather than being extracted from plants or animals.

Antibiotics and 'Wonder Drugs'

► Alexander Fleming checks the growth of bacteria on a culture dish, having inoculated the spots on the dish with penicillin.

▼ A tropical swamp, breeding ground for the Anopheles mosquito, whose bite spreads malaria (see opposite).

1928 marked one of the greatest advances in medicine – and it happened almost by accident.

British scientist Alexander Fleming was studying bacteria in his laboratory at St Mary's Hospital, London. He used the standard laboratory technique of growing the bacteria on **nutrient jelly** in small round dishes, called culture dishes. Somehow, airborne spores of a mould (fungus) got onto one plate and **contaminated** it. As the mould grew, Fleming noticed that bacteria nearby were killed off.

Further work revealed that a substance produced by the mould could affect several types of bacteria that caused common infections. The mould's scientific name was *Penicillium notatum*, and so Fleming called this new substance penicillin.

Large-scale Production and Testing

The next task was to make pure penicillin in large quantities for tests on people. This was achieved by two scientists at Oxford University, Howard Florey and Ernst Chain. The first tests during the Second World War were successful. The era of antibiotic drugs had begun.

Soon similar antibiotics were discovered that attacked other disease-causing bacteria. In 1943, American **microbiologist** Selman Waksman discovered streptomycin, another powerful antibiotic made by a mould that grows in soil. (Waksman had invented the name antibiotic in 1941.)

Antibiotics Today

Today, we have dozens of antibiotic drugs. Prescribing them can be complicated. Some attack many types of bacteria and are called broad-spectrum. Others have more limited effects and are known as narrow-spectrum. Some types of bacteria become resistant to specific antibiotics, so others are tried against them. Some people are sensitive to one type of antibiotic, and so another type must be chosen for them.

▲ Jonas Salk checks bottles of microbes in his University of Pittsburg laboratory, in 1955. He developed the Salk vaccine against the dreaded disease polio, saving thousands from death or crippling deformity.

Did You Know?

Malaria is one of the world's major diseases. For many years the most effective drug against it was quinine. But quinine is not the result of the chemist's laboratory, it is a natural substance found in the bark of the cinchona tree. It was first used in purified form in about 1630. From about 1934, synthetic drugs such as amodiaquine have been used against malaria.

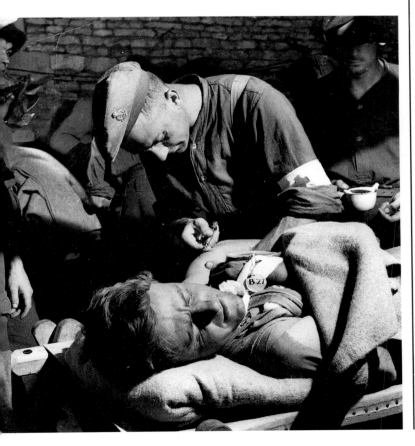

◄ Injured troops receive injections of antibiotics during the Second World War. By preventing secondary infection of wounds, possibly millions of lives were saved.

Advances in Surgery

During the early and mid 20th century, while patients were benefiting from the increasing numbers of drugs, there were also strides forward in surgery. These had been made possible by the discoveries of Lister (page 27) and by the development of **anaesthesia** in the previous century.

Anaesthetics

Arabian doctors had used drugs such as opium, from the opium poppy, and hyoscyamus, from plants such as henbane and deadly nightshade, to dull the senses during surgery. Alcohol was another drug that put patients into a **stupor**. But for centuries, there was no good way to prevent the terrible pain of cutting during an operation. There were no anaesthetics to put patients to sleep, so operations had to be performed very quickly.

A dentist, Horace Wells of Connecticut, USA, tried using the fumes given off by liquid ether as an anaesthetic. Around 1845 he extracted teeth from his patients in this way. But the first successful demonstration of ether as an anaesthetic was given by William Morton at

▲ John Snow, the first professional anaesthetist in Britain, used this type of chloroform inhaler to put patients to sleep in the 1850s.

▶ Robert Hinckley's painting of Morton's first public demonstration of ether as a general anaesthetic, in the 'Ether Dome' of the Massachusetts General Hospital.

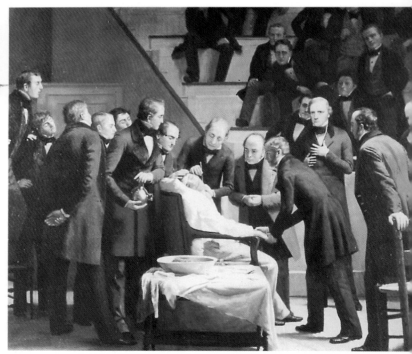

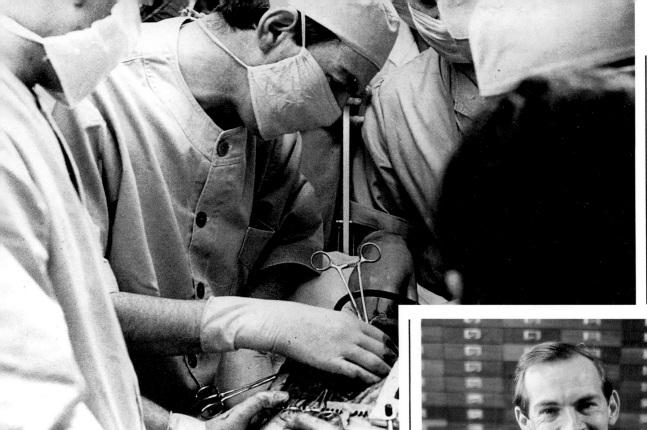

Massachusetts General Hospital USA, in October 1846. He removed a growth from the neck of a patient.

By 1847, **chloroform** was being used instead of ether, since it was more controllable and had fewer bad effects. Since this time, anaesthesia has become an important branch of medicine. The anaesthetist is a vital part of the surgical team and has many techniques at his or her disposal. Anaesthetics put the patient to sleep (general anaesthesia) or deaden feeling in one part of the body (local anaesthesia).

Surgery and Technology

Anaesthesia allowed surgeons to take more time over their work, since the speed of the operation was less important now that the patient could be made unconscious. Surgery became more adventurous, and new and longer operations were developed.

▲ Pioneering surgeon Christiaan Barnard, operating on an anaesthetized patient. He carried out the world's first heart transplant in 1969 at Cape Town, South Africa.

X-rays and Radiology

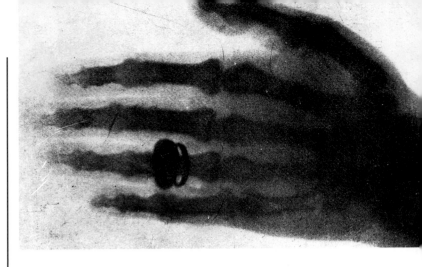

In 1895, Professor of Physics Wilhelm Röntgen was experimenting with a new device called the vacuum-tube, at Wurzburg in Germany. He discovered that it gave off invisible rays that could pass through less dense materials, like wood, but not through dense substances such as metals. He had little idea of the nature of the rays, so he called them X-rays.

Röntgen soon noticed that the rays passed through the body's flesh and muscle, but not through the denser cartilage or bone. That December he took a picture of his wife's hand, in which the bones stood out white. It was the first X-ray image, or radiograph, of the body.

▲ Wilhelm Röntgen and the X-ray of his wife's hand. Denser parts like the bones (and the ring!) show clearly. In modern X-rays the denser parts are white against a dark background.

▶ An early X-ray clinic at about the end of the 19th century. The risks of strong X-rays had not yet been realized, hence the lack of protective screens or special clothing.

Did You Know?

The first patient to be helped by X-rays was Eddie McCarthy, an American from Dartmouth. In 1896 his broken arm was set using information from an X-ray photograph of his arm bones.

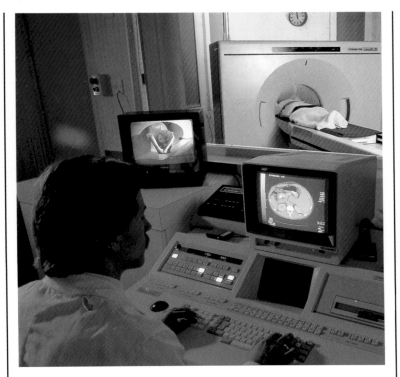

◀ A CAT scan in progress. The monitor screen in front of the radiographer shows a 'slice' through the abdomen of the patient.

The Dangers of X-rays

During the early research into X-rays, some workers suffered from skin ulcers, anaemia of the blood, and certain types of cancers. Such conditions were also found to be caused by exposure to the naturally radioactive substances radium and thorium, discovered by Marie and Pierre Curie in 1898. It was shown that high doses of X-ray **radiation** harmed living tissues and brought on disease. Doctors turned this into an advantage by using carefully controlled doses of radiation to kill off diseased tissues such as cancers. This technique is known as radiotherapy.

The Developing Science of Radiology

Doctors soon realized that the new X-rays could be used to picture the inside of the body, to locate foreign bodies or breaks in bones. At the turn of the century a technique was developed in which patients swallowed bismuth, a substance that shows up white on X-rays. A series of X-rays, taken as the bismuth moved through the digestive system, revealed any blockage or other problem in the gullet, stomach or intestines.

In 1922 a similar technique was developed for the lungs, by Jean Sicard and Jacques Forestier. An injection of a substance containing **iodine** showed up on the X-ray and outlined any abnormal parts in the air passages.

From these early days, the branch of medicine known as radiology has made many advances. There are now various scanning techniques that use different types and strengths of X-rays, such as CAT scanners that see inside the body (page 40).

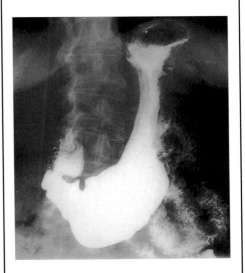

▲ An X-ray of the stomach, using swallowed barium (which shows up bright white) to outline its shape more clearly, as a J-shaped bag. The bones of the spine show up faintly behind.

6: THE MEDICAL SYSTEM TODAY

Check-Ups and Tests

▶ A visit to the dentist is advised every 6–12 months. The dentist looks for early signs of tooth decay, gum disease or other problems, which can be treated more effectively before they worsen.

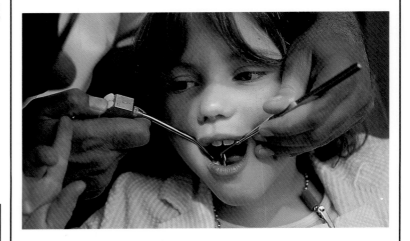

The Quality of Life

One aim of medicine is to preserve and lengthen life. Another aim is to ease suffering. These two aims do not always go together. For example, a baby may be born badly deformed. Many operations would be needed to give a chance of survival. But it is not certain if treatment will succeed, or if it does, what sort of life will be in store afterwards.

Or an old, frail person may be diagnosed as having a serious disease, that could be curable – but only with extensive treatment, that has many side-effects. Again, the patient's 'quality of life' is in question.

In such cases the friends, relatives, doctors, and the patients themselves, must decide about very difficult questions. Is it worth giving treatment? If so, for how long? What are the chances of survival? Will the person be able to live a worthwhile life, able to enjoy happiness and contentment, without too much pain and suffering?

Detecting disease early, even before it causes outward signs of illness, is beneficial for all. Medical science has developed many techniques that check for certain diseases or give early warning signs of trouble, even when the person has no symptoms. This is known as primary screening or having a check-up.

Who to Screen, and What For

We cannot screen for every illness. Most people get better on their own from minor illnesses. Only certain more serious conditions, such as some cancers and heart problems, have early signs that can be detected rapidly and effectively. The test itself must not pose too many risks to the people tested.

We cannot screen everyone. It may be people of a certain age who are most at risk from a certain illness, or men rather than women, or someone with a family history of the condition. So the screening is usually concentrated on a particular target group – those who are at risk.

Diagnostic Tests

Once a person has **symptoms** of illness, he or she visits the doctor. The doctor asks questions about the current problem and past health. This is known as 'taking a medical history'.

The doctor may carry out diagnostic tests that can be done quickly in a clinic. For example, a urine sample could be tested with a chemically-coated 'dipstick', for abnormal urine contents.

If the problem cannot be identified, or if it needs more detailed investigation, then further diagnostic tests are arranged. These range from taking a blood sample for later laboratory analysis, to attending hospital for an ECG or a scan (page 40).

(page 40).

The Pap Test

In 1928, the Greek-American scientist George Papanicolaou, working in a New York team, developed a test for cancers of the uterus (womb) and cervix (neck of the womb). A 'smear' sample from the womb lining could be checked under the microscope for early signs of disease, including pre-cancer cells. If detected early, there is an excellent chance of cure.

Today, the Pap test is widely used in many countries, to screen for cervical disease. Guidelines vary, but in general each woman has a test every year or few years, from the age of about 25, or if taking the contraceptive pill, or after childbirth.

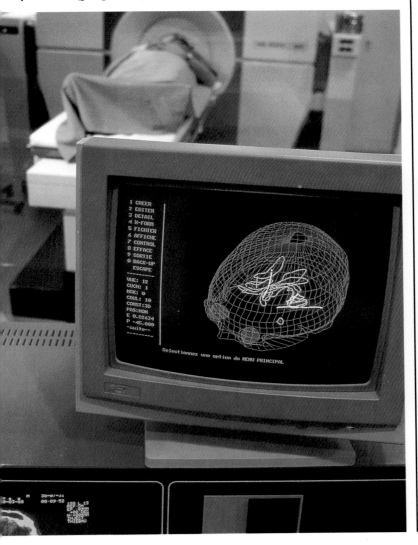

◄ The CAT scanner reveals a brain tumour, which the computer displays in green on its 3D 'map' of the head. The tumour can be removed before it enlarges and causes more serious problems.

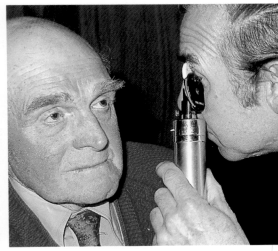

▲ An eye examination can also reveal general problems, such as high blood pressure, from the condition of the nerves and vessels visible in the retina, at the back of the eye.

Electronic Eyes

▼ Thermography detects the temperatures of body parts. It can pick up 'hot spots' such as abnormal growths. Nuclear magnetic resonance (NMR) imaging shows the body's response to a strong magnetic field, made by huge magnets (below right). The NMR scan (bottom right) shows soft tissues in detail – even the plum the patient was eating!

ECGs and EEGs

Some problems inside the body can be detected on its surface. As the heart pumps, and the muscles pull, and the brain thinks, they produce tiny bursts of electricity from muscular and nerve action. These bursts travel through the body, and their 'echoes' can be detected on the skin by sensitive electrical equipment.

The ECG, or electrocardiograph, measures the electrical signals from the heart. The signals are displayed as wavy lines on paper or a TV screen. Their pattern tells the doctor if the heart is enlarged, as in heart failure, or if parts of it are diseased or injured, as after a heart attack.

The EEG, or electro-encephalograph, detects electrical signals from the brain – brain waves. Its wavy lines give information about abnormality or injury, as caused by a stroke or a condition such as **epilepsy**.

Seeing Inside the Body

Over the past 30 years, one of the greatest areas of medical progress has been in non-invasive

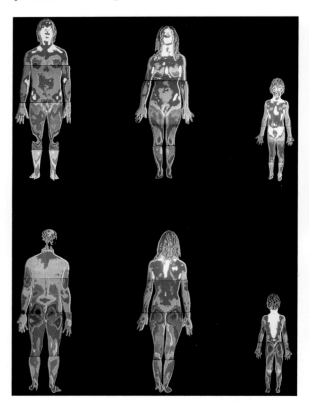

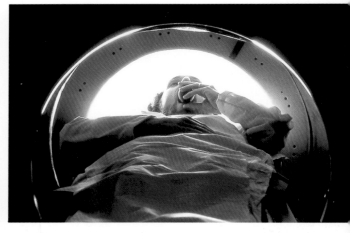

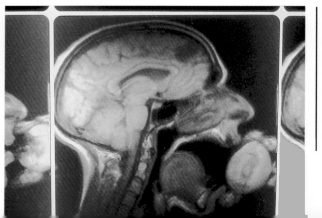

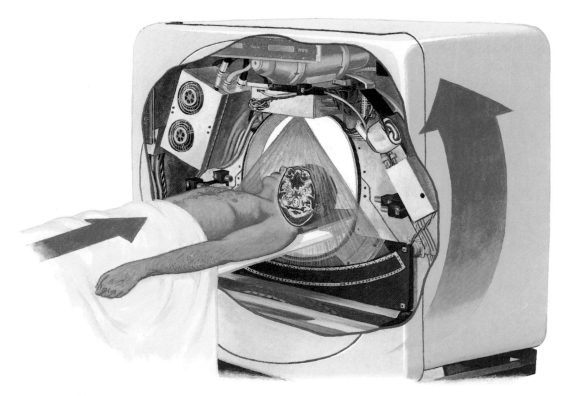

imaging. This means looking into the body, and seeing in detail the structure and workings of its internal organs, without having to cut it open or 'invade' it in some other way. X-rays (page 36) were the first method of this type. Today there are more than a dozen techniques, and the clarity of the images is improving all the time. Computers are used to control the scanners, and to process, combine and colour the images, so that doctors can see more clearly if there are any problems.

▲ The CAT scanner is like a rotating X-ray camera that revolves around the body in a giant drum. The X-rays are extremely weak and harmless, yet the combined image of a 'slice' through the body is very detailed.

◄ This pregnant woman is having an 'ultrasound' scan. High pitched sound waves are beamed through the body, they are then processed by the computer into an image. Ultrasound helps to check that the developing baby is healthy. These scans show the baby's foot (lefthand screen) and his arm and fist (middle screen).

Drug Treatments

There are thousands of drugs. Some are extracted from natural sources such as plants, but an increasing number are made in the chemist's laboratory. Dozens of new drugs are brought onto the market each year.

Problems in Prescribing

Prescribing the correct drug can be very complicated. First, it must be a drug that will act against the illness in question. Second, it must be the right dose, for the person and the severity of the illness. But this is not all.

There must be no contra-indications. These are conditions or diseases that the patient has, or has had in the past, which could cause problems when the drug is given. For example, some drugs should not be prescribed for people who have kidney disease, or epilepsy.

Side-effects

There are also side-effects to consider. Sometimes the side-effects of a powerful drug could be worse than letting the disease run its course. A few people are sensitive to certain drugs. Also a drug taken for a short time may interfere with one already being taken for a long-term condition, such as **asthma** or diabetes.

▼ Developing a new drug takes years and costs millions. Only 1 in 1,000–10,000 of the possible drugs tried, will make it through all the tests and go onto the market.

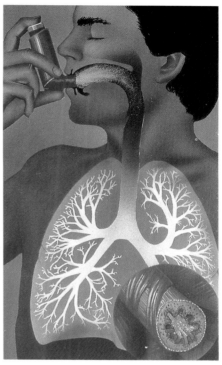

◄ The way the body deals with a drug can give indications to illness. Samples of blood, urine, saliva and other body fluids may be analyzed to find out how fast the drug is being broken down, and into which end-products.

Learning from Mistakes

New drugs have to be thoroughly tested on laboratory animals and on cells grown in the laboratory, before the first trials are done on human volunteers. Gradually, if a new drug passes all the tests, it goes into general use.

Even so, problems with a drug often do not emerge until years later, when many thousands of people have taken it. In the 1950s **amphetamines** were widely used as 'slimming pills'. But people soon came to realize that their stimulant effects, and problems of addiction, far outweighed their usefulness. They were banned. Today, they are taken illegally as 'speed', 'pep pills' and 'uppers'.

▼ Part of a drug's effectiveness depends on how and where it enters the body. Aerosol inhalers for controlling asthma deliver the drug as a fine mist into the airways – precisely where it is needed.

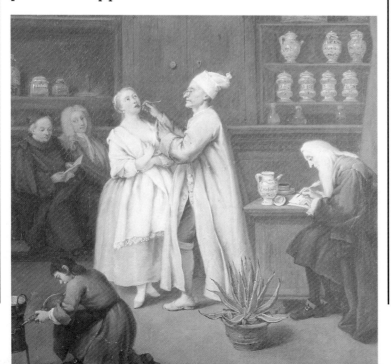

◄ The old-time apothecary's shop was filled with minerals and processed parts of plants and animals. However, the prescriber did not have the in-depth scientific back-up knowledge which is available from books and computers to today's doctors.

Surgery, Trans-plants and Implants

Today's surgeon can select from a multitude of instruments and hi-tech equipment. Most surgeons specialize in one region of the body. The cardiac surgeon operates on the heart and **great blood vessels**, and the neurosurgeon concentrates on the brain and nerves.

A complicated operation today usually involves a surgical team. There are the chief and assistant surgeons, the anaesthetist, the nursing staff, and specialist operators of complex machinery such as heart-lung machines and X-ray equipment.

Transplants

A transplanted part is taken from one person, the donor, and put into the body of another, the recipient. The donor may be a living person, such as a relative who donates a kidney to a family member with kidney failure. Or the donor has died, usually as the result of an accident such as a car crash. The donor, or the relatives of a dead person, must give permission for the parts to be used as transplants.

Heart transplants were in the news for many years in the 1970s. In the 1980s they became

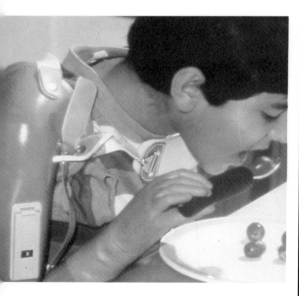

▲ The myo-electric limb helps to replace a limb lost through accident or disease. Small sensors on the skin of the stump detect tiny electrical signals from muscles inside it. These are amplified and fed to electric motors and other devices that move the arm.

▶ A Starr-Edwards type heart valve (size 9), and an X-ray image of it in position in the living heart.

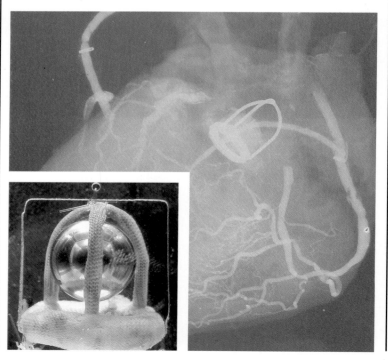

◀ The surgical team in operation. The anaesthetist's trolley is towards the bottom, with bottles of anaesthetic gas. Surgical instruments are laid out on the trolley near the top of the picture.

Transplants and Implants ▼

1.	Metal Plate	15.	Elbow
2.	Plastic eye	16.	Wrist
3.	Rubber ear	17.	Knuckles
4.	Fillings	18.	Liver
5.	Jaw	19.	Kidney
6.	Teeth	20.	Pancreas
7.	Voice-box	21.	Insulin pump
8.	Lung	22.	Hip
9.	Arm	23.	Metal bone rods
10.	Pacemaker	24.	Knee
11.	Valve	25.	Metal shin plates
12.	Heart	26.	Leg
13.	Breast implant		
14.	Shoulder		

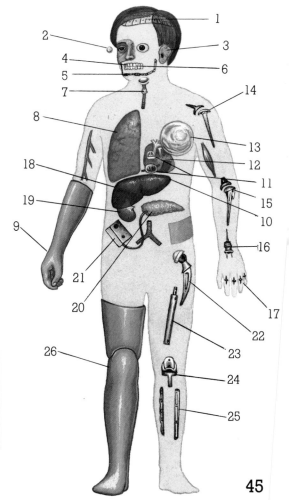

more common. Many other parts are also transplanted, including heart and lungs, liver, kidney, pancreas, bone marrow, the cornea of the eye, larynx (voicebox), trachea (windpipe), and of course blood in a blood transfusion.

A major problem is that the recipient's body fights against the transplant, as if it were a foreign invader. In the 1980s, new types of **immunosuppressive** drugs, were developed. These damp down the defending immune system, so that there is less chance of rejecting the transplant.

Implants

Artificial body parts such as metal false teeth have been used for centuries. But over the past 40 years, many new spare parts have been developed. These usually rely on finding the right substance, which the body will not reject, such as special metals and plastics.

Treating
the Mind

The diagnosis and treatment of mental illness – illness of the mind – has a very patchy history.

The Ancient Chinese, Greeks and Indians knew that some illnesses did not involve physical problems, with symptoms such as a growth or swelling. The illnesses seemed to be based in people's minds. The only signs were in the way they behaved, and handled their emotions and reactions. Early views of mental illness were often linked to magic, superstition and being possessed by evil spirits.

For centuries during the Middle Ages, people with mental illnesses were locked away from society and forgotten. In many lunatic asylums the conditions were horrific. There was little hope of receiving treatment or being freed. The public paid to come and see the 'mad people', even to taunt them into a frenzy.

The Beginnings of Psychiatry

In the late 19th and early 20th centuries, some doctors became interested in the diagnosis and treatment of mental illnesses. One of the first who tried to explain such illnesses, and devise treatments, was Viennese physician Sigmund Freud. He founded several areas of psychology – the scientific study of how the mind works, and why we act and behave as we do.

▶ Modern life's many stresses, such as overwork and worries about jobs and money, can place a great strain on the mind. Like a bone put under too much strain, the mind can 'snap', leading to mental illness.

Freud was also involved in the early stages of modern psychiatry, which is the study, diagnosis and treatment of mental illnesses. In particular, he began the approach known as psychoanalysis.

Within a few years, several of Freud's colleagues had disagreements with him, and they left to establish their own schools of psychology. Alfred Adler, an Austrian, departed in 1911. Carl Jung, who was the first President of the International Psychoanalytic Association, left in 1913. Both have left their mark on modern psychiatry.

Since its turbulent start, psychiatry has become a major branch of medicine. But there are still many different theories and ideas about why mental illnesses occur, and how they should be treated. Given its short past, the history of psychiatric medicine is probably only just beginning.

What is Mental Illness?

Most people cope with life's ups and downs. Although they are sometimes very sad, or worried, they shrug off such feelings and behave again in a reasonable and sensible way.

In a mental illness, the person's mind and thinking become abnormal. He or she cannot cope with daily life and shows strange behaviour, odd moods, and irrational reactions.

Mental illnesses are often difficult to identify and explain because human behaviour is so complicated and variable. Also, what people regard as 'normal behaviour' varies from place to place, and from one time to another.

In general, if the illness is less severe, and the person realizes that there is a problem, this is called a 'neurosis'. Examples are bouts of severe depression, or the compulsion to wash hands after touching any object. In a 'psychosis', the person loses touch with reality and does not recognize that there is something wrong.

◀ Sigmund Freud thought that when we dream our unconscious thoughts reveal our worries and anxieties. By confronting and analysing these unconscious thoughts Freud thought that we could overcome our problems.

7: AROUND THE WORLD

China and the East

Chinese Medicine

Chinese medicine is probably the oldest in the world. Today, Chinese medical care still relies on the traditions of past centuries, called *Chung-i*. These are used alongside methods learned from India and, more recently, with new technologies and drugs from the West.

There is a strong belief in China that health in the body is based on the harmony of opposing forces. These are called *yin* (which is cool and 'female') and *yang* (hot and 'male'). Illness happens when the forces are out of balance, and the traditional treatments have healing energies that work to restore the balance. Other forms of treatment in China are acupuncture, massage, and special healing exercises.

Barefoot Doctors

China's population is so great that one fifth of the people of the world live in that one country. This means there is a lack of funds to provide enough fully-trained doctors. The term barefoot doctor is used for part-time health workers who are trained for about six months, in both traditional and Western medicine. They concentrate on

▲ The symbolic balance in a healthy body of yin and yang, represented by the dark and light colours.

► Traditional remedies on display in a street market in Yangshuo, southern China. Many traders have extensive knowledge of how to prepare the remedies, and for which illnesses they are suitable.

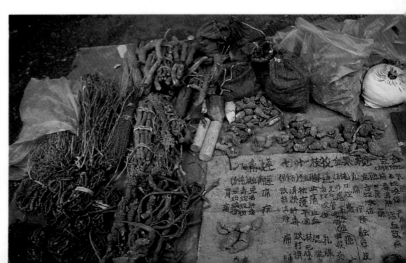

problems such as coughs, colds, lack of healthy food, and infection due to poor sanitation. They also give advice about pregnancy and childbirth, childcare, preventing illness and birth control. They have been very successful, and there are now over 1,300,000.

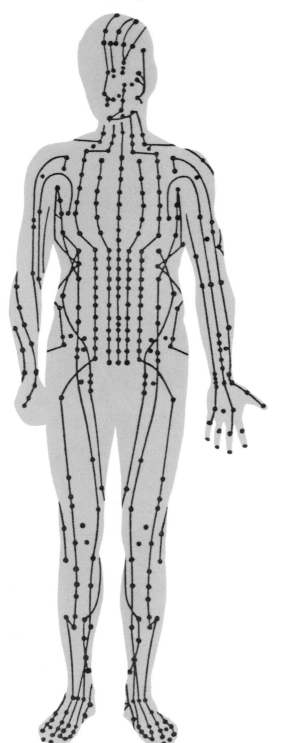

Medical Facts: China

One way of viewing the effectiveness of a medical system is to measure the life expectancy of the people. This is the average age to which people live. Another method is to assess the infant mortality. This is the numbers of babies dying just before, at, or soon after birth. See also boxes on pages 50, 53 and 55.

● In 1949, life expectancy in China was about 30 years. By the 1980s it was 68 years.

● Infant mortality is around 35 deaths per 1,000 babies.

● There are some 300,000 registered acupuncturists and **herbalists**.

● There is 1 qualified doctor per 2,000 people.

● There is 1 hospital bed per 500 people.

◀ The acupuncture channels, or meridians, are said to carry *chi* energy through the body. Needles in the insertion points either speed or slow this energy flow.

▼ In both China and Japan acupuncture is a form of medicine.

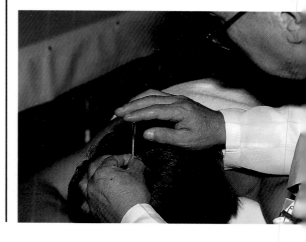

India and the Middle East

▶ Health workers advise on family planning methods, as part of the national campaign to slow the increase in the population. Too many people will stretch food supplies, water and sanitation systems and also health services.

Medical Facts: India

● Life expectancy for women is about 54 years, and for men 55 years.

● Infant mortality is around 110 deaths per 1,000 babies.

● Birth control is seen as an important way to reduce the population, so putting less strain on the food supply and medical services.

● There is 1 qualified doctor per 3,600 people.

● There is 1 hospital bed per 1,600 people.

See also boxes on pages 49, 53 and 55.

▶ Shanty towns, such as this one in India, are the enemy of good health and proper medical care. Flies spread germs from the open sewers onto food, and the drinking water is contaminated.

Ayurveda is the traditional medicine of India. It stretches back at least 3,000 years. It has been passed down in verses and sacred poetry, and is based on centuries of experience with herbs and other medicinal substances. There are over 14,000 **dispensaries** in India, where practitioners advise patients and supply traditional cures.

Most Indian doctors are trained in both traditional and Western medicine. However in many places, especially the cities, traditional techniques are regarded less highly, and many doctors practise mainly Western-style medicine.

A street medical trader in Karwar, southern India. In areas where there are no officially qualified doctors, traditional traders help to give advice and supply medicines.

Money brings improved medical facilities. Some of Saudi Arabia's oil wealth has been put towards health care, as with the King Khaled Eye Hospital.

The herb *Rauwolfia* has been used for more than 2,000 years in India. Its roots contain the medical drug reserpine, which helps to calm the brain and heart, and lower blood presure.

In Pakistan, traditional medicine is known as *Unani-tibb*. It is carried out by doctors who are trained at medical schools and who also study Western methods.

Rich and Poor

The Middle East is another area with a long tradition of healing. Today it is a region of contrasts. Some countries have become rich from selling oil, and have bought expertise and up-to-date equipment from the West. Neighbouring poor countries, without oil, struggle to provide clean water and proper sewage disposal, in attempts to prevent diseases such as **cholera** and **dysentery**. They also lack money to teach their people about basic hygiene.

Africa

▶ A traditional diviner from southern Africa. She holds a special object which helps to concentrate and direct her spiritual powers.

▲ A *binjar* or traditional healer from southern Sudan, holding a bottle of medicine during a healing ceremony.

Healing by the Spirits

The traditional medicine of many African groups is centred on a person with special powers, the healer. This is usually a man, who has been chosen early in life, and served a long period of training with his predecessor. He learns how to make and use medicines, and how to make contact with the spirit world during healing ceremonies. The spirits pass their powers through him, and so he is able to cure the sick. Over nine-tenths of medicines used in this way come from plants.

Many of these traditional treatments have been passed by word of mouth and there are no written records. Knowledge about them is in danger of disappearing, as societies change and adopt Western ways. Traditional healers have become part of the State medical system in some countries, such as Zimbabwe.

Hunger and Malnutrition

The main problems causing disease in Africa are lack of food, poverty, and poor sanitation. Lack of food means malnutrition, people develop illnesses due to vitamin shortage. Food for everyone is a priority.

The main aims of the health services are to control tropical diseases caused by **parasites**, such as malaria, to grow enough food for everyone to eat a healthy diet, to wipe out

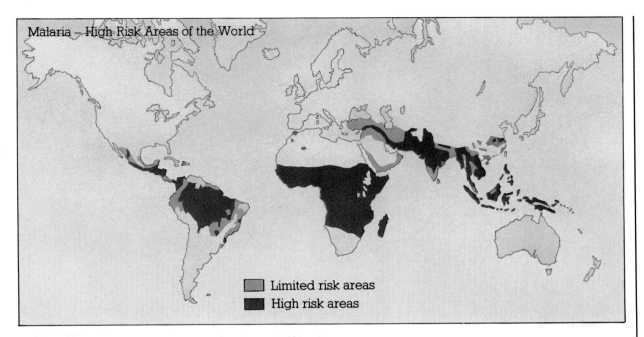

Malaria – High Risk Areas of the World

Limited risk areas
High risk areas

▲ Malaria represents one of the world's most serious health problems (see pages 32–3).

◄ Medical care pales against the basic human need for food. These children from famine-stricken Ethiopia have a poor diet that makes them more susceptible to illness.

diseases (using drugs donated by the rich countries), and to immunize more children against infections, as is now done in the West.

Where You Are, and Who You Are

In Africa, as in many regions, medicine varies even within a country. Access to health care is important. Are facilities available in your area, and if they are, can you use them? You might be prevented from doing so because of your cultural or ethnic group, or your lack of money.

Medical Facts: Kenya

● Life expectancy for women is about 61 years, and for men 57 years.

● Infant mortality is less than 50 deaths per 1,000 babies.

● There is 1 qualified doctor per 10,000 people.

● There is 1 hospital bed per 1,000 people.

See also boxes on pages 49, 50 and 55.

The Americas

▶ In remote areas, people rely on themselves for medicines. This man from Ecuador grows medicinal herbs in his garden, 12,000 feet high in the Andean Mountains.

▲ The Mandan Medicine Man, Mah-To-He-Ha ('Old Bear'), painted by the famous North American artist George Catlin in 1832.

The various native groups of people in North, Central and South America each had their own traditional types of medicine. Today, traditional medicine is still used in remote areas, such as the Amazon rain forests and Andean Mountains. But in most other places, modern Western-style medicine has taken over.

North American Indians

Many Indian groups believe that illness is due to forces from the spirit world, especially those connected with animals, plants and nature. Their view of medicine is tied in with their view of nature, and of living with the natural world and trying to conserve it, rather than destroying it. For example, the spirits might be displeased because an animal had been killed at the wrong time, and so they would bring the curse of illness.

When a North American Indian became ill, the first person to consult was the group's herbalist. If medicinal herbs did not work, then a **diviner** might be called in to try to find the cause by divining, or hand-trembling.

The main healer was someone who would smoke, sniff or chew on certain drug-containing

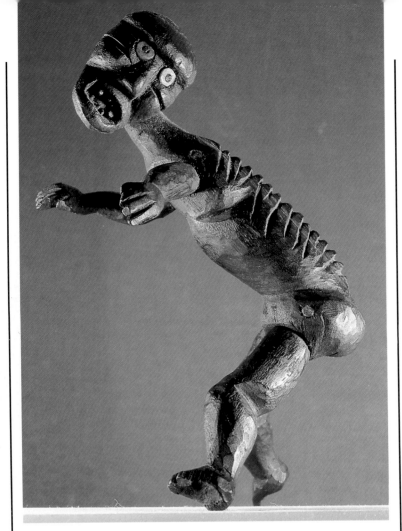

◄ In some Inuit groups of the American far north, small figures and statues are made as offerings to the spirits, for a long and healthy life. This figurine, called a tupilaq, is intended to bring harm to others!

Medical Facts: Brazil

● Life expectancy for women is about 67 years, and for men 62 years.

● Infant mortality is less than 70 deaths per 1,000 babies.

● There is 1 qualified hospital doctor per 2,300 people.

● There is 1 hospital bed per 280 people.

See also pp. 49, 50, 53.

Medical Facts: Bolivia

● In contrast to Brazil, in Bolivia the life expectancy is about 50 years, and infant mortality is more than 120 deaths per 1,000 babies.

plants, and enter a trance to communicate with the spirits. The drug-induced state supposedly had special healing powers.

South American Indians

Like the Indians in North America, those in South America rely mainly on medicinal plants for healing. One famous group are the Kallawaya, from Bolivia. In the Aymara language, their name means 'carrying medicine on the shoulder'. They travel with bags of dried herbs, diagnosing and treating illnesses and holding medical ceremonies.

In many cultures, such as some Indian groups, the knowledge of medicine and healing gives the doctor a special type of power and influence in the community. Such knowledge and skills are therefore kept as well-guarded secrets.

Did You Know?

Some of the greatest disease **epidemics** have been due to mild illnesses which have been introduced to a new group of people, who have no resistance. During the invasion of Mexico by Cortes and his followers in 1520, hundreds of thousands of Mexican Indians died from diseases such as smallpox and measles, brought by the invaders. Some experts estimate that in the 100 years following the European invasion of the Americas, over 50 million American Indians perished from such diseases.

8: MEDICINE IN THE FUTURE

The Coming Challenges

Medicine continues to face many challenges. Some, like malaria, have probably been around since history began. Others, such as **AIDS**, have a very short history.

Environmental Causes of Illness

Each year, about six million people in the world develop cancers. In these diseases, body cells suddenly go out of control. They fail to do their usual jobs. They begin to multiply and form growths, and they spread around the body.

For many years the causes of cancers were a mystery. But more and more cancers are being linked with our environment. Certain chemicals such as **dioxins**, tobacco smoke and **asbestos** can trigger cancerous changes in the body. So can the wrong types of food, too much radiation, and many other factors.

New Diseases

In the early 1980s, a new disease was recognized, first in the USA and then in other countries. It attacked the body's immune system. This is our body's ability to resist disease and

Facts and Feats

Over the centuries, smallpox has probably disfigured and killed more people than any other disease. About 60 million people died from it in the 18th century alone. In 1967, the World Health Organization began a campaign to wipe out this disease, by vaccination and other measures. In 1979, it succeeded. The world officially became 'smallpox-free'.

► Clean air, like good food and pure water, is a pre-condition for health. Some of the air pollutants we pour into the atmosphere today, may be found to cause slowly-developing illnesses in years to come.

◄ The foxglove flower (centre) has been used for centuries as a medicinal plant. Its various medical drug ingredients, such as digoxin and digitoxin, help the heart to beat more smoothly and regularly. The reason for this property was discovered by an 18th-century English doctor, William Withering.

▲ Certain diseases tend to run in families or be more common in some ethnic groups. A genetic counsellor is a medical specialist who can advise on the risks of children being affected.

illness, without which we cannot fight back against illness. The disease was named AIDS (Acquired Immune Deficiency Syndrome), and it was discovered to be caused by a virus, HIV – Human Immunodeficiency Virus.

At the end of the 1980s, the World Health Organization estimated that 600,000 people around the world suffered from AIDS. But millions more have the virus, especially in Africa, and they will eventually develop the disease. No one has yet recovered from AIDS. But we are working on drugs to cure it.

Millions of dollars have been spent on AIDS, and into drugs, research and vaccines for it. Much of the money, skills and time devoted to AIDS would otherwise have been spent on other illnesses. From AIDS research other beneficial medicine has been discovered. The course of medical progress has been changed by something too small to be seen except under the most powerful microscope. The late 20th century will go down in history as the era of AIDS.

Success Story

Many cancers are now being treated more successfully. This is due to earlier detection, and to better treatments combining drugs, radiotherapy and surgery. For example, acute lymphatic leukaemia is a cancer-type blood disease of children. In the late 1950s, only 1 sufferer in 25 was cured. By the late 1970s, it was 1 sufferer in 2. The cure rate for Hodgkin's disease, a cancer of the **lymph glands**, has also improved over the same time, from 2 sufferers in 5, to 4 in 5.

Healing the World

► These Romanian children are infected with AIDS. As yet, we have no cure for AIDS so we must concentrate on prevention. These children do not have access to expensive hospitals, equipment, technology and medicine. They have only the very bare medical care.

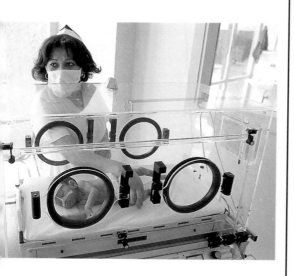

▲ In contrast to the Romanian children, this newborn British baby is being looked after with great care, using an incubator and other specialist equipment.

In the future, our medicine of today will be part of history. People may look back at our times and wonder: Why did we have to cut people open to cure them? Why did we struggle so to understand mental illness? And especially, why were millions of people in some parts of the world dying of hunger, yet in other parts of the world, great amounts of money were being spent on drugs and surgery for just a few people?

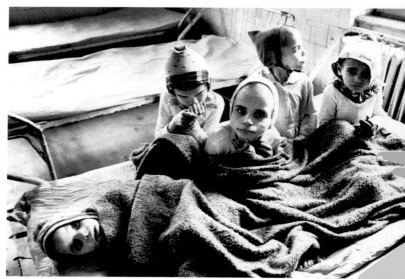

Basic Needs

Better health for millions of people depends not on better medical care, but on basic human needs. They need enough good food, clean water, and proper living conditions and sanitation. These are not so much medical problems, but challenges for society as a whole. They are complicated by wars, religions and politics.

Immunization Programmes

The Smallpox campaign has shown that we can succeed in ridding the world of a disease. Immunization programmes are one of the most effective ways of doing this. But this work requires great quantities of money, for health workers, vaccines, equipment and publicity. Greater amounts of money are currently being spent on developing and making weapons.

Prevention Is Better Than Cure

This old saying has never been more true. Slowly, people – particularly in rich countries – are realizing that they can, and should, take better care of themselves. This means eating healthy food, not being overweight, taking plenty of exercise, and other preventative measures. It also involves cleaning up our environment and reducing our use of dangerous and polluting chemicals.

Medicine For All?

Today, as in the past, medicine is linked to people's attitudes to health and illness, and to their traditions and beliefs. Its progress relies on the research and discoveries made by scientists, and also on how much money we are willing to spend on medical care. This is not a decision for doctors and patients, but a question for the whole of society.

Holistic Health

Some people believe that modern Western-style medicine has a major failing. It tends to treat just a particular symptom, or a part of the body. It does not take into account the 'whole person', including the person's mind, emotions, outlook, attitude and feelings towards life. Holistic medicine has this approach, and it has become more popular. Some experts predict that it will be a guiding force in the future of medical care.

◀ Nature has supplied us with so many of our medicines and cures. Yet in many areas, such as the Amazon forest, people are destroying plants and animals before they can be investigated for medicinal properties.

Glossary

AIDS: Acquired Immune Deficiency Syndrome, a disease spread by a virus (HIV) that attacks the body's immune system; this means that other, more common diseases can be deadly because the body cannot fight off the infection.

amphetamines: laboratory-made drugs used to stimulate the body.

anaemia: a blood disorder in which there is not enough of the oxygen-carrying substance haemoglobin in the blood.

anaesthesia: lack of feeling, or numbness brought on by a drug or substance. In a general anaesthesia the person becomes completely unconscious.

anatomist: someone who studies the structure of the body.

anatomy: the structure of the various parts of the body, such as the nerves, bones and so on.

animalcules: an early word for tiny animals and other organisms.

anthrax: a disease that affects humans and cattle, involving spots, sores and lung infections.

antibiotics: drugs that fight infection by **bacteria**.

antiseptics: substances that kill or disable **bacteria**.

arteries: the tubes that carry blood from the heart to all parts of the body.

asbestos: a mineral used in insulation, fire proofing and in many other ways, but which can cause cancer.

asthma: a condition that causes periodic difficulty in breathing, affecting the lungs.

bacteria: living things which are only visible under a microscope. They are neither plants nor animals. Some are harmless but others cause infections and are called germs.

bacteriology: the study of **bacteria**.

blood vessels: tubes known as **arteries, capillaries** and veins that carry blood around the body.

capillaries: tiny blood vessels only visible under a microscope. They join small **arteries** to veins.

cells: the microscopic building blocks from which all complex living things are made.

cellular pathology: the study of the change that cells undergo when they become abnormal, infected, cancerous or **diseased** in some way.

chloroform: a gas used as an **anaesthetic** to deaden the senses.

cholera: a digestive disease which causes extreme diarrhoea. It is caused by **bacteria** and spread in unclean water and food.

contaminated: someone or something carrying harmful chemicals or germs that could cause illness is said to be contaminated.

cultures: in medicine, growing germs or other cells in special laboratory conditions. The cultures are usually grown on **nutrient jelly** in glass containers.

Dark Ages: also known as the Middle Ages, the period of European history from about the 5th–13th centuries, when there was little progress in arts and sciences including medicine.

diabetes: a condition caused by excess of sugar in the blood due to lack of the hormone insulin.

diagnosis: detecting which disease or illness a person is suffering from.

dioxins: very poisonous substances formed when certain plastics and other substances are made.

diphtheria: an infectious disease that causes the throat to be narrowed by a tough growth that blocks the air passages and makes breathing difficult.

diseased: a similar word to illness or sickness.

dispensary: a place where drugs and other medicines are given to patients.

diviner: a person who can locate the source of water by touch, sensation or movement passed through a rod, stick or bar, called a divining rod.

dysentery: an infection caused by bacteria or similar germs, involving extreme diarrhoea, digestive upsets and pains in various parts of the body.

embryology: the study of the development and growth of babies in the womb.

epidemic: when a disease is caught by a great number of people at one time, over a large area such as a continent.

epilepsy: a condition of the nervous system which may cause fits, seizures or convulsions.

fermenting: when a substance breaks down with the aid of micro-organisms over a period of time, to produce other simpler substances.

gout: a disease which affects certain joints in the body, making them swell up so that movement is difficult and painful.

G.N.P.: the gross national product is the amount of money, goods and services that a country produces every year. This is one way of measuring the wealth of a nation.

great blood vessels: the main **arteries** and veins that join to the heart.

herbalist: a person who uses plants and herbs as medicines to relieve or cure symptoms.

hydraulic: a mechanism or machine worked by pressurised liquids, such as the brakes of a car or a digging arm of an earth mover.

immunisation: when the body becomes **immune**, or able to fight off a particular disease (usually an infection), either by having the disease itself or having an **inoculation**.

immunosuppressive: a drug that damps down the body's **immune** system.

Industrial Revolution: A period of social and economic change beginning in Britain in the 1760s. It involved the change from working mainly in homes and on farms to working in factories and using large machines.

inoculation: injecting disabled forms of the germs that cause a certain disease into a person in order to build up resistance to that disease and make the body **immune**.

iodine: a liquid used as an **antiseptic**.

lymph glands: parts of the body that store and process lymph, a watery substance that flows around the tissues, helping to distribute nutrients, collect wastes and fight infections.

malaria: an infectious disease carried by a type of female mosquito, that sucks blood and so passes on the disease. It is a recurring illness that consists of fever and hot and cold sweats along with other symptoms.

mental illness: an illness of the mind that affects a person's behaviour, emotions and reactions to other people.

microbes: very small organisms such as **bacteria** and **viruses**, only visible under a microscope.

microbiologist: a person who studies microscopic organisms such as **viruses, bacteria** and tiny animals and plants.

micro-structure: an incredibly small pattern of cells, that can only be seen with a microscope.

Neanderthal: a type of human that lived from about 120,000 to 40,000 years ago. Neanderthals were shorter and stockier than people today, they had large brains and used tools and fire.

Nobel Prize: prizes awarded yearly by the Nobel Academy in Stockholm founded by Alfred B. Nobel, the Swedish scientist who discovered dynamite. The prizes are in many subjects such as literature, physics, medicine and peace.

nutrient jelly: a jelly that contains many nutrients, used in laboratories to grow organisms.

osteopath: a person who treats muscle pain, swollen joints and similar problems mainly through manipulation and massage.

oviducts: the tubes through which eggs from female mammals (including humans), travel to the womb.

papyrus: a reed plant that was pressed and made into paper by the Ancient Egyptians.

parasites: creatures that live on or in other animals, using the larger 'host' animal for food and as a home. This causes damage or illness to the host.

pathology: the study of how disease affects the body.

physiology: the study of the way living things work.

physiotherapist: a person who treats illness by physical methods such as exercise.

psychiatry: the study and treatment of illnesses of the mind (**mental illness**).

radiation: a type of energy in the form of invisible waves or particles, that can damage living tissues. Radiation can come from various sources such as certain types of rocks, the sun or X-ray machines.

Renaissance: a period of European history from the early 14th–late 16th century. The name means 're-birth' and marks the change from the Middle Ages to the Modern Age. The re-birth refers to the revival of arts, literature, politics, trade, sciences and medicine.

sperm: sex cells made by the male which fertilise the egg made by the female, so that it develops into a baby.

stupor: a state of mind or body in which a person acts in a lazy, slow or confused way.

surgical instruments: scissors, forceps (tweezers), scalpels (sharp knives) and many other instruments used by doctors and surgeons during operations (surgery).

symptoms: a feature of an illness or disease that the sufferer notices.

tissues: tissues make up various parts of the body. They consist of similar types of **cells** working together to do a particular job.

tuberculosis (TB): an infection by **bacteria** affecting mainly the lungs, causing fever, coughing and general ill health.

vaccination: giving the body a disabled form of the germs which cause an illness (see **inoculation**) so that the body builds up resistance and becomes **immune**.

virus: the smallest kind of living organism, that live inside cells. Some viruses can cause disease and illness in humans.

Index

A **Bold** number shows the entry is illustrated on that page. The same page often has writing about the entry too.

acupuncture **19,49**
Adler, Alfred (Austrian psychologist) 47
Aesculapius *see* Asklepios
African medicine 52-3
AIDS 56-7
Alcaemon (Greek physician) 12
alcohol 6, 17
American Indian medicine 54-5
amodiaquine (anti-malarial drug) 33
amphetamines 43
amputation **5**
anaemia 25
anaesthetics **34-5**
anatomy **8** 13, **20**-1, 23
animalcules 26
anthrax 27
antibiotics 11, 16, **32-3**
apothecary's shop **43**
Aristotle (Greek physician) 12, **13**
art therapy **30**
Asklepios (Greek priest-physician **13**
asthma **43**
at risk group screening 38
Australian medicine 7
Avicenna *see* Ibn Sina
Ayurveda (Indian medicine) 50

bacteria 16, 23, 26
bacteriology 27, 30, 31, **32-3**
Banting, Frederick (English physician) **30**
barefoot doctors, Chinese 48-9
barium 'meal' **37**
Barnard, Christiaan (South African surgeon) **35**
Best, Charles (English physician) **30**
bile 15
binjar (African healer) **52**
Black Death, the 16, 17
blood 11, 12, 13, **16**, 24-5, 28-9
    groups 31
    pressure **7**
    samples **43**
Bolivia, medical facts 55
Bologna medical school 20, **21**
bones 5, 10, 11, 17, 36

brain, the 13, 29
    see also mental illness
Brazil, medical facts 55

cancers 7, 22, 29, 38, 56, 57
Canon of Medicine (Ibn Sina) 17
cardiologists (heart specialists) 9, 44-5
castor oil 11
CAT scanners **37, 39, 41**
cell theory 29
cellular pathology 29
Celsus (Greek physician) 12
cervical smear test 39
Chain, Ernest (British scientist) 32-3
check-ups, medical 38-9
Chen Ch'uan (Chinese physician) 19
childhood illnesses 8, 9, 31, 57
chinchona bark (quinine) 25, 33
Chinese medicine **8**, 19, 20, 46, 48-9
Le Chirurgien Dentiste, ou Traite des Dents (Fauchard) 25
chloroform **34-5**
colchicine (painkiller) 19
confidentiality, principle of 15
Constantine 17, **20**
constipation 11
consultants 9, 44-5
contra-indications, drug 42
Cosmos see saints, healing
coughs 7
cowpox 26
Curie, Marie and Pierre 37

Damian *see* saints, healing
De Contagione et Contagiosis Morbis (Fracastoro) 23
De Humani Corporis (Vesalius) 21
De re Medica (Celsus) 12
deadly nightshade 34
dentists 5, 24, **25**, 34, **38**
    Roman false teeth **12**
depression, mental 4
diabetes 19, 30
diagnosis 14, 29
    screening tests 38-9
diet 4, 6, 11, 15, 52-3
diseases 5, 13, 22, 23, 27, 56-7
    see also malaria
dissection (cutting open) 12, **21**, **28**, 29
diviners **52**, 54

doctors 5, 9, 10, 15
    Roman 12-13
    specialists 9, 44-5
'Doctrine of Signatures' **19**
dreams and illness 13, 31, 46-7
drugs 5-9, 16, 17, 25, 45
    19th-20th century 30-3
    chemical 23, 30-1, **42**
    herbal 18, **19**, **48**-9, **51**, **54-5**, **57**
    treatment 42-3, 56-7

Ebers papyrus, the 11
ECGs (electrocardiographs) 39, 40
EEGs (electro-encephalographs) 40
Egyptian medicine, ancient **10-11**
Ehrlich, Paul (German bacteriologist) 31
electronic eyes 40-1
'elements', the four 15
embryology (study of eggs) 28
emergency medical care **9**
Empedocles (Greek physician) 12, **13**
environmental causes of illness 56
epidemics *see* Fracastoro; plague, the
ether **34-5**
exercise 4
Exercitatio Anatomica de Motu Cordis et Sanguinis in Animalibus (Harvey) 24
experiments 22-3, 27
eye diseases 11, 19, 29, **39**, **51**

Fallopio, Gabriello (Italian physician) 21
false teeth, Roman **12**
family doctors 9
famines 5, **53**, 58
'Father of Medicine' *see* Hippocrates
Fauchard, Pierre (French physician) 24, **25**
Fernel, Jean François (French physician) **22-3**
Fleming, Alexander (British physician) **32**
Florey, Howard (British scientists) 32-3
Fracastoro, Giorlamo (Italian physician) 23
Freud Sigmund (Austrian psychiatrist) 31, **47**

Galen (Roman physician) **13**, 20, 21

genetic diseases **57**
germs *see* bacteria
ginseng root **19**
GPs (General Practitioners) *see* family doctors
Greek medicine, ancient 12, **13, 14-15**, 46

Harvey, William (English physician) **24-5**
health care 4-9
  the cost of 7, 8, **9**
  keeping healthy 6-7
  levels of 8-9, 49, 50, 53, 55
  WHO 5, 56, 57
  workers 5
heart, the 4, 11, 12, 13, 57
  Harvey's ideas on **24-5**
  transplant/implants **35, 44, 45**
heat therapy, medieval **19**
henbane 34
Henle Jakob (German physician) 29
herbal medicine 18, **19, 48-9, 51, 54**-5
Hippocrates (Greek physician) 13, **14-15**
  Hippocratic oath 15
Hodgkin, Thomas (English physician) **26**
holistic health 59
hospitals 5, 7, 9, 17
  beds available 49, 50, 53, 55
  medieval **18**
  Roman **12**-13
humours, the four 15
hygiene 13, 15, 27, 51, 52-3
hyoscyamus 34

Ibn Sina (Persian physician) 17
Ibn Zakaiyya Ar-Razi, Abu-Bakr Muhammad (Persian doctor) 17
Imhotep (Egyptian god) **10**, 11
immune system 26, 56-7
immunization 31, 56, 58
implants **44, 45**
Indian medicine 46, 50-1
  American 54-5
infant mortality 49, 50, 53, 55
inoculation 26
insulin 30
  pump **45**
iodine 37
Islamic Empire, medicine in the 16-17
Jenner, Edward (English physician) **26**

Jung, Carl (Austrian psychologist) 47
Kallawaya (Bolivian Indians) 55
Kenya, medical facts 53
kidneys, the 29
  see also transplants
Kitab al-hawi (Rhazes) 17
Koch, Robert (German physician) 26, **27**
Kom Ombo (Egyptian) sculpture **10-11**

laboratory technicians 9
Landsteiner, Karl (Austrian physician) 31
Leonardo da Vinci **20**, 21
leprosy **19**
leukaemia 57
life expectancy 49, 50, 53, 55
Lister, Joseph (British physician) 26, **27**
lung diseases 19, **43**

magic *see also* African/American/Chinese/Indian medicine; religion and medicine
Mah-To-He-Ha (medicine man) **54**
malaria 5, 17, 25, **32**, 33 56
  World map **53**
Malpighi, Marcello (Italian physician) **28**
medical books 14, 15, 19, 22, 23, 24, 25
medical records 15, 25
medical schools 14-15, 20-1
medical services 5, 8-9
  in the future 56-9
  levels of care 8-9, 48-55, 58
  today 38-47
Medicare/Medicaid 8
medicine 4-9
  in the 19th and 20th centuries 30-7
  today 38-47
  in ancient times 10-15
  around the world 48-55
  in the future 56-9
  in medieval times 16-21, 46
  scientific beginnings 22-9
mental illness 4, 5, 8, 31, **46**, 58
  art therapy **30**
  Sigmund Freud **47**
Methodus Curandi Febres (Sydenham) 25

Michelangelo 21
microbes *see* bacteria
microscopes 28-**9**
Middle Ages, medicine in the 16-21, 46
mind, the *see* mental illness
miner's lung 22
Montpellier medical school 20
moral code, doctors' 15
Morton, William (American anaesthetist) **34-5**
muscles 13, **20**-1
myo-electric limb **44**

Nei Ching (Chinese medical book) 20
nerves 13, 44
neurosis 46
neurosurgeons 44
Nightingale, Florence **27**
NMR (Nuclear Magnetic Resonance) **40**
non-invasive imaging 40-1
Nuba wrestlers (Sudan) **4**
nurses 5, 9
  Florence Nightingale **27**

observation 14, 22-3, 25
obstetricians 9
occupational diseases 22
operations *see* surgery
Opere Ippocrate e Galeno (Constantine) **17**
opium 11, 25, 34
orthopaedics 9
osteopaths 5

Padua medical school 21, 22
paediatricians 9
painkillers 11, 19, 25
Papanicolaou, George (Greek-American scientist) 39
Paracelsus (German/Swiss physician) **22**, 23
Paré, Ambroise (André) **23**
Pasteur, Louis (French physician) **26**
pathology 12, **21**, 23, 26, **28**
  cellular 29
Pen T'saokangmu (Chen Ch'uan) 19
penicillin 11, **32-3**
Persia, famous physicians of 17
phlegm 15
physiology 21, 23
physiotherapists 5

plague, the 16, 17
polio 33
poppy sap 11, 25, 34
pregnancy 9, **16**, 21, **41**, 49
preventative medicine 6-7,
   14-15, 59
psychology and psychiatry **30**,
   31, **46**, **47**
psychosis 46
pulse rate 8, 21

'qualities of life', the four
   ancient 15
quality of life, the 38
quinine 25, 33

radiology and raidiotherapy
   36-7
Ramazzini, Bernardino (Italian
   physician) 22
Reed, Walter (American
   physician) 30, **31**
religion and medicine 11, 13,
   15, **17**, **18**-19
   see also African/American/
     Chinese/Indian medicine
Renaissance, medicine in the
   20-1, 22
Rhazes (Persian physician) 17
Roman medicine, ancient **12**, **13**
Röntgen, Professor Wilhelm
   (German radiologist) **36**

saints, healing **17**
Salk, Jonas (American
   microbiologist) **33**
Salvarsan (drug) 31
Sanctorius, Sanctorio (Italian
   physician) 21
scans **37**, **39**, **41**
'scientific' medicine 12, 22-9
screening 38-9
side-effects, drug 15, 42
smallpox 26, **55**, 56, 58
Smith papyrus, the 11
smoking 6, **7**
Snow, John (British anaesthetist)
   34
'spare parts' surgery **44**, **45**
specialists 9, 44-5
sperm cells 29
suicide 4
Sumatra, medicine in **6**
suntan 4
superstition *see* African/
   American/Chinese/Indian
   medicine;

religion and medicine
surgery 7, 9, **23**, 31
   20th century 34-**35**
   amputation **5**
   surgical instruments **10-11**,
     17, 22
   transplants and implants 44-5
Susruta (Indian physician) 17
Sydenham, Thomas (English
   physician) 24, **25**

tannic acid 11
temperature, body 21, 25, 40
thermography 40
transplants 44-**5**
Traumdeutung, die (Freud) 31
trepanning 10-**11**
trephining *see* trepanning
tuberculosis (TB) 5, 27
tupilaq (Inuit Indian figurine) **55**

'ultrasound' scans **41**
UN (United Nations), WHO 5
Unani-tibb (Pakistani medicine)
   51
Universa Medicina (Fernel) 23
USA, medicine in the 7, 8

vaccination 26, 32-3
van Leeuwenhoek, Antony
   (Dutch physician) 28-9
Vesalius, Andreas (Belgian
   physician) 21
Virchow, Rudolf (Prussian
   physician) 29
virus, HIV 56-7
   see also bacteriology
von Behring, Emil (German
   bacteriologist) 31
von Hohenheim, Philip Bombast
   see Paracelsus

Waksman, Selman (American
   biologist) 33
Wells, Horace (American
   dentist) 34
WHO (World Health
   Organization) 5, 56, 57
'wonder drugs' 7, 32-3

X-rays 9, **36**, **37**

yellow fever 30
yin and yang **48**